PYTHON DATA SCIENCE

SCIENCE

Learn Python in a Week and Master it

---

7 Days Crash Course

An hands-on introduction to big data analysis and data mining, a project-based guide with practical exercises (BOOK 3)

Computer Programming Academy

Table of Contents

Introduction

Congratulations on purchasing *Python Data Science: An hands-on introduction to big data analysis and data mining, a project-based guide with practical exercises (Book 3)* and thank you for doing so.

The following chapters will discuss the fundamental concepts of data science technologies that can be used to analyze raw data and generate predictions and resolve business problems. There are 7 chapters in this book, crafted specifically to help you master all the data analysis concepts required to produce meaningful insight from a large volume of data in just a week (7 chapters for 7 days).

The first chapter of the book will help you understand the importance of data science technologies in our everyday lives ranging from weather forecasting to cyber attacks. You will also learn different types of data and various data science implementation strategies. A detailed overview of the "Team Data Science Process", which is a data science lifecycle widely used for projects that require the deployment of applications based on artificial intelligence and/or machine learning algorithms, has been provided in the second chapter. You will learn the objectives defined at each of the 5 stages of this lifecycle along with the deliverables that are created at the end of each stage.

The third chapter is all about big data and big data analytics. You will learn the 5 Vs of big data and the 3 important actions required to gain insights from big data. You will also learn the different steps involved in big data analysis and some of its applications in healthcare, finance, and other industrial sectors. The chapter entitled "Basics of Data Mining" will provide an explicit overview of the data mining process and its applications. You will also learn the advantages and challenge of the data mining process in resolving real world data problems. Some of the most widely used data mining tools that are being used by data analysts are also explained.

The fifth chapter deals exclusively with some of the key data analysis frameworks, including ensemble learning, decision trees and random forests. These are the most popular machine learning algorithms that are capable of processing a large volume of unstructured and unorganized data to generate useful insights and predictions. You will learn the advantages and disadvantages of these frameworks as well as the steps required to implement random forest regression on a real life dataset. Chapter six, entitled "Data Analysis Libraries", is a deep dive into the functioning of different Python based data analysis libraries including IPython, Jupyter Notebook, Pandas, Matplotlib among others. You will learn how these powerful libraries can be used to analyze real life data set with select open source sample dataset that you can download and gain hands-on experience with.

The final chapter of this book will explain to you how the data analysis helps resolve business issues using customer and/or predictive analytics. Customer analytics is at the heart of all marketing activities and is an umbrella term used for techniques such as "predictive modeling", "data visualization", "information management", and "segmentation". You will learn the important concept of marketing and sales funnel analytics as well as the three main types of predictive models to analyze customer behavior. The concepts of exploratory analysis of customer data and personalized marketing have been explained in detail, along with some of their industrial applications. To make the best use of this book, We recommend that you download the free resources provided in this book and perform hands-on exercises to solidify your understanding of the concepts explained. The skillset of data analysis is always in demand, with a lot of high pay job opportunities. Here's hoping this book will take you a step closer to your dream job!

Day 1: Introduction to Data Science

In the world of technology, Data is defined as "information that is processed and stored by a computer". Our digital world has flooded our realities with data. From a click on a website to our smart phones tracking and recording our location every second of the day, our world is drowning in the data. From the depth of this humongous data, solutions to our problems that we have not even encountered yet could be extracted. This very process of gathering insights from a measurable set of data using mathematical equations and statistics can be defined as "data science". The role of data scientists tends to be very versatile and is often confused with a computer scientist and a statistician. Essentially anyone, be it a person or a company that is willing to dig deep to large volumes of data to gather information, can be referred to us data science practitioners. For example, companies like Walmart keeps track of and record of in-store and online purchases made by the customers, to provide personalized recommendations on products and services. The social media platforms like Facebook that allow users to list their current location is capable of identifying global migration patterns by analyzing the wealth of data that is handed to them by the users themselves.

The earliest recorded use of the term data science goes back to 1960 and credited to Pete Naur, who reportedly used the term data science as a substitute for computer science and eventually introduced the term "datalogy". In 1974, Naur published a book titled "Concise Survey of Computer Methods", with liberal use of the term data science throughout the book. In 1992, the contemporary definition of data science was proposed at "The Second Japanese-French Statistics Symposium", with the acknowledgment of emergence of a new discipline focused primarily on types, dimensions and structures of data.

"Data science continues to evolve as one of the most promising and in-demand career paths for skilled professionals. Today, successful data professionals understand that they must advance past the traditional skills of analyzing large amounts of data, data mining, and programming skills. In order to uncover useful intelligence for their organizations, data scientists must

master the full spectrum of the data science life cycle and possess a level of flexibility and understanding to maximize returns at each phase of the process".

– University of California, Berkley

An increasing interest by business executives has significantly contributed to the recent rise in popularity of the term data science. However, a large number of journalists and academic experts, do not acknowledge data science as a separate area of study from the field of statistics. A group within the same community considers data science is the popular term for "data mining" and "big data". The very definition of data science is up for debate within the tech community. The field of study that requires a combination of skill set including computer programming skills, domain expertise and proficiency in statistics and mathematical algorithms to be able to extract valuable insight from large volumes of raw data is referred to as data science.

Importance of Data Science

Data Science is heavily used in Predictive analysis. For example, weather forecast requires collection and analysis of data from a variety of sources, including satellites, radars, and aircraft, to build data models that are even capable of predicting the occurrence of catastrophes of the nature such as hurricanes, tornadoes and flash floods. Another branch of data science is "big data and big data analytics", which are used by organizations to address complex technical problems as well as for resource management. You will learn more about big data later in this book. The ability of data science to analyze the challenges facing any and all industrial sectors like healthcare, travel, finance, retail, and e-commerce has contributed significantly to its increasing popularity among business executives.

Data science has made the use of advanced machine learning algorithms possible, which has a wide variety of applicability across multiple industrial domains. For example, the development of self-driving cars that are capable of collecting real-time data using their advanced cameras and sensors to create a map of their surroundings and make decisions pertaining to the speed of the vehicle and other driving maneuvers. Companies are always on the prowl to better understand the need of their customers. This is now achievable by gathering the data from existing sources like customer's order history, recently viewed items, gender, age and demographics and applying advanced analytical tools and algorithms over this data to gain valuable insights. With the use of machine learning algorithms, the system can generate product recommendations for individual customers with higher accuracy. The smart consumer is always looking for the most engaging and enhanced user experience, so the companies can use these analytical tools and algorithms to gain a competitive edge and grow their business.

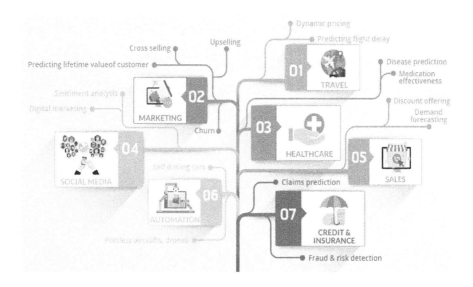

The ability to analyze and closely examine Data trends and patterns using Machine learning algorithms has resulted in the significant application of data science in the cybersecurity space. With the use of data science, companies are not only able to identify the specific network terminal(s) that initiated the cyber attack but are also in a position to predict potential future attacks on their systems and take required measures to prevent the attacks from happening in the first place. The use of "active intrusion detection systems" that are capable of monitoring users and devices on any network of choice and flag any unusual activity serves as a powerful weapon against hackers and cyber attackers. While the "predictive intrusion detection systems" that are capable of using machine learning algorithms on historical data to detect potential security threats serves as a powerful shield against the cyber predators. Cyber attacks can result in a loss of priceless data and information resulting in extreme damage to the organization. To secure and protect the data set, sophisticated encryption and complex signatures can be used to prevent unauthorized access. Data science can help with the development of such impenetrable protocols and algorithms. By analyzing the trends and patterns of previous cyber attacks on companies across different industrial sectors, Data science can help detect the most frequently targeted data set and even predict potential future cyber attacks. Companies rely heavily on the data generated and authorized by their customers but in the light of increasing cyber attacks, customers are extremely wary of their personal information being compromised and are looking to take their businesses to the companies that are able to assure them of their data security and privacy by implementing advanced data security tools and technologies. This is where data science is becoming the saving grace of the companies by helping them enhance their cybersecurity measures.

Over the course of the past 20 years, Data trends have drastically changed, signaling an ongoing increase in unstructured data. It is estimated that by the year 2020, "more than 80% of the data that we gather will be unstructured". Conventionally, the data that we procured was primarily structured and could be easily analyzed using simple business intelligence tools but as reflected in the picture below unstructured and semi-structured data is on the rise. This, in turn, has warranted the development and use of more powerful and advanced analytical tools than the existing business intelligence tools that are incapable of processing such large volume and variety of data. We need more sophisticated analytical tools and algorithms that are capable of processing and analyzing unstructured and semi-structured data to provide valuable insights.

Types of Data

Let us look at different types of data so you can choose the most appropriate analytical tools and algorithms based on the type of data that needs to be processed. Data types can be divided into two at a very high level: qualitative and quantitative.

Qualitative data – Any data that cannot be measured and only observed subjectively by adding a qualitative feature to the object it's called as "qualitative data". Classification of an object using unmeasurable features results in the creation of qualitative data. For example, attributes like color, smell, texture, and taste. There are three types of qualitative data:

- **"Binary or binomial data"** – Data values that signal mutually exclusive events where only one of the two categories or options is correct and applicable. For example, true or false, yes or no, positive or negative. Consider a box of assorted tea bags. You try all the different flavors and group the ones that you like as "good" and the ones you don't as "bad". In this case, "good or bad" would be categorized as the binomial data type. This type of data is widely used in the development of statistical models for predictive analysis.

- **"Nominal or unordered data"** – Data characteristics that lack an "implicit or natural value" can be referred to as nominal data. Consider a box of M&Ms, you can record the color of each M&M in the box in a worksheet, and that would serve as nominal data. This kind of data is widely used to assess statistical differences in the data set, using techniques like "Chi-Square analysis", which could tell you "statistically significant differences" in the amount of each color of M&M in a box.

- **"Ordered or ordinal data"** – The characteristics of this Data type do have certain "implicit or natural of value" such as small, medium, or large. For example, online reviews on sites like "Yelp", "Amazon", and "Trip Advisor" have a rating scale from 1 to 5, implying a 5-star rating is better than 4 which is better than 3 and so on.

Quantitative data – Any characteristics of the data that can be measured objectively are called as "quantitative data". Classification of an object in using measurable features and giving it a numerical value results and creation of quantitative data. For example, product prices, temperature, dimensions like length, etc. There are two types of quantitative data:

- **"Continuous Data"** – Data values that can be defined to a further lower level, such as units of measurement like kilometers, meters, centimeters, and on and on, are called the continuous data type. For example, you can purchase a bag of almonds by weight like 500 g or 8 ounces. This accounts for the continuous data type, which is primarily used to test and verify different kinds of hypotheses such as assessing the accuracy of the weight printed on the bag of almonds.

- **"Discrete Data"** – numerical data value that cannot be divided and reduced to a higher level of precision, such as the number of cars owned by a person which can only be accounted for as indivisible numbers (you cannot have 1.5 or 2.3

cars), is called as discrete data types. For example, you can purchase another bag of ice cream bars by the number of ice cream bars inside the package, like four or six. This accounts for the discrete data type, which can be used in combination with a continuous data type to perform a regression analysis to verify if the total weight of the ice cream box (continuous data) is correlated with the number of ice cream bars (discrete data) inside.

Data science strategies

Data science is mainly used in decision-making by making precise predictions with the use of "predictive causal analytics", "prescriptive analytics", and machine learning.

Predictive causal analytics –"predictive causal analytics" can be applied to develop a model that can accurately predict and forecast the likelihood of a particular event occurring in the future. For example, financial institutions use predictive causal analytics based tools to assess the likelihood of a customer defaulting on their credit card payments, by generating a model that can analyze the payment history of the customer with all of their borrowing institutions.

Prescriptive analytics - The "prescriptive analytics" are widely used in the development of "intelligent tools and applications" that are capable of modifying and learning with dynamic parameters and make their own "decisions". The tool not only predicts the occurrence of a future event but is also capable of providing recommendations on a variety of actions and its resulting outcomes. For example, the self driving cars gather driving related data with every driving experience and use it to train themselves to make better driving and maneuvering decisions.

Machine learning to make predictions – To develop models that can determine future trends based on the transactional data acquired by the company, machine learning algorithms are a necessity. This is considered as "supervised machine learning", which we will elaborate on later in this book. For example, fraud detection systems use machine learning algorithms on the historical data pertaining to fraudulent purchases to detect if a transaction is fraudulent.

Machine learning for pattern discovery – To be able to develop models that are capable of identifying hidden data patterns but lack required parameters to make future predictions, the "unsupervised machine learning algorithms", such as "Clustering", need to be employed. For example, telecom companies often use the "clustering" technology to expand their network by identifying network tower locations with optimal signal strength in the targeted region.

Machine Learning Vs Data Science

Data science is an umbrella term that encompasses machine learning algorithms. Here are some basic distinctions between the two terms.

Data components

Data science pertains to the complete lifecycle of data and involves a variety of components including "ETL" (Extract, Transform, Load) pipeline to collect and classify data, Data visualization, distributed computing, machine learning, artificial intelligence, Data engineering, dashboards, and System deployment introduction and environment among other components.

Machine learning models are provided input data and

contain various components including: data separation, data exploration, problem-solving and appropriate model selection among other features.

Performance measures

Data science has no standard for performance measurement and is determined on a case-by-case basis. Typically, performance measures are an indication of Data quality, Data timeliness, Data accessibility, Data visualization capability and data query capability.

Machine learning models have standard performance measures, with each algorithm having a measure to indicate the success of the model and describing the given training data set. For example, in "linear regression analysis", the "Root Mean Square Error (RME) serves as an indication error(s) in the model.

Development method

Data science project implementations are carried out in defined stages with project milestones that must be reached to fulfill set goals and targets within the constraints of time and resources. Machine learning projects are research-based and start with a hypothesis that is expected to be verified within the constraints of available data.

Data visualization

In data science projects, data is visualized with the use of standard graphical representation, such as bar graphs and pie charts. Machine learning not only uses the standard graphical representation tools to visualize the data but it also uses mathematical models of the training data set.

Programming language

The most popular programming language used in Data science projects are "SQL", "PERL", and certain data framework specific languages such as "Java for Hadoop" and "Scala for Spark". The most widely used programming languages in machine learning algorithms are "Python" and "R- programming". For data exploration activities, "SQL" can be used with the machine learning algorithms.

Input data

Data science projects use "human consumable data", which can be easily read and analyzed by humans using and analytical tools and technologies.

Machine learning algorithms require highly classified and labeled training data set.

Business Intelligence Vs. Data Science

Data science, as you have learned by now, is an interdisciplinary approach that applies mathematical algorithms and statistical tools to extract valuable insights from raw data. On the other hand, Business Intelligence (BI) refers to the application of analytical tools and technologies to gain a deeper understanding of the current state of the company as it relates to the company's historical performance. Simply put BI provides intelligence to the company by analyzing their current and historical data, whereas data science is much more powerful and capable of analyzing the humongous volume of raw data to make future predictions.

An avalanche of qualitative and quantitative data flowing in from a wide variety of input sources has created a dependency on data science for businesses to make sense of this data and use it to maintain and expand their businesses. The advent of data science as the ultimate decision-making tool goes to show the increasing data dependency for businesses. In a number of Business, intelligence tasks could potentially be automated with the use of data science driven tools and technologies. The ability to gather insights using these automated tools from anywhere across the world, with the use of the Internet, will only propel the use of "centralized data repositories" for everyday business users.

Business intelligence is traditionally used for "descriptive analysis" and offers retrospective wisdom to the businesses. On the other hand, Data science is much more futuristic and used for "predictive and prescriptive analysis". As data science seeks to answer questions like "Why the event occurred and can it happen again in the future?", Business intelligence focuses on questions like "What happened doing the event and what can be changed to fix it?". It is this fundamental distinction between the "Ws" that are addressed by each of these two fields, that sets them apart.

The niche of business intelligence was once dominated by technology users with computer science expertise. However, Data science is revamping the Business intelligence space by allowing non-technical and core business users to perform analytics and BI activities. Once the data has been operationalized by the data scientists, the tools are easy to use for the mainstream business corridor and can be easily maintained by a support team, without needing any data science expertise. Business intelligence experts are increasingly working hand in hand with the data scientist to develop the best possible data models and solutions for the businesses. Unlike Business intelligence that is used to create data reports primarily key performance indicators and metrics dashboards and provide supporting information for data management strategy, Data science is used to create forecasts and predictions using advanced tools and statistics and provide supplemental information for data governance. A key difference between Data science and business intelligence lies in the range and scale of "built-in machine learning libraries", which empower everyday business users to perform partially automated or automated data analysis activities. Think of data science as business intelligence on steroids that is set to turn the business analysis world into a democracy!

Features	Business Intelligence (BI)	Data Science
Data Sources	Structured (Usually SQL, often Data Warehouse)	Both Structured and Unstructured (logs, cloud data, SQL, NoSQL, text)
Approach	Statistics and Visualization	Statistics, Machine Learning, Graph Analysis, Neuro- linguistic Programming (NLP)
Focus	Past and Present	Present and Future
Tools	Pentaho, Microsoft BI, QlikView, R	RapidMiner, BigML, Weka, R

Data Science Vs Data Analysis

The terms of data science and data analytics are often used interchangeably. However, these terms are completely different and have different implications for different businesses. Data science encompasses a variety of scientific models and methods that can be used to manipulate and analyze structured, semi structured, and unstructured data. Tools and processes that can be used to make sense of gather insight from highly complex, unorganized and raw data set falls under the umbrella of data science. Unlike data analytics that is targeted to verify a hypothesis, data science boils down to connecting data points to identify new patterns and insights that can be made use of in future planning for the business. Data science moves the business from inquiry to insights by providing a new perspective into their structured and unstructured data by identifying patterns that can allow businesses to increase efficiencies, reduce costs and recognize the new market opportunities. Data science acts as a multidisciplinary blend of technology, machine learning algorithm development, statistical analysis, and data inference that provides businesses with enhanced capability to solve their most complex business problems. Data analytics falls under the umbrella of data science and pertains more to reviewing and analyzing historical data to put it in context. Unlike data science, data analytics is characterized by low usage of artificial intelligence, predictive modeling and machine learning algorithms to gather insights from processed and structured data using standard SQL query commands. The seemingly nuanced differences between data analytics and data science can actually have a substantial impact on an organization.

Review Quiz

Answer the questions below to verify your understanding of the concepts explained in this chapter. The answer key can be found at the end of the quiz.

1. Name the process of gathering insights from a measurable set of data using mathematical equations and statistics.

2. What kind of systems are capable of monitoring users and devices on any network of choice and flagging any unusual activity, serving as a powerful weapon against hackers and cyber attackers.

3. The type of numerical data value that cannot be divided and reduced to a higher level of precision is called ____.

4. What are the different types of qualitative data?

5. The ____ tool can predict the occurrences of a future event as well as provide recommendations on a variety of actions and its resulting outcomes.

6. What type of data values can be defined to a further lower level, such as units of measurement like kilograms, grams, and so on?

7. ____ is used to create executive level data reports, primarily key performance indicators, and metrics dashboards.

8. What data component serves as a pipeline to collect and classify data?

9. _____ uses the standard graphical representation tools to visualize the data, but it also uses mathematical models of the training data set.

10. ____ refers to the application of analytical tools and technologies to gain a deeper understanding of the current state of a company as it relates to its historical performance.

Answer Key

1. Data Science
2. Active intrusion detection systems
3. Discrete data type
4. Binary or binomial data, Nominal or unordered data, Ordered or ordinal data
5. Prescriptive analytics
6. Continuous data type
7. Business intelligence
8. ETL" (Extract, Transform, Load)
9. Machine learning
10. Business Intelligence

Day 2: Data Science Lifecycle

The most highly recommended lifecycle to structured data science projects, the "Team Data Science Process" (TDSP). This process is widely used for projects that require the deployment of applications based on artificial intelligence and/or machine learning algorithms. It can also be customized for and used in the execution of "exploratory data science" projects as well as "ad hoc analytics" projects. The TDSP lifecycle is designed as an agile and sequential iteration of steps that serve as guidance on the tasks required for the use of predictive models. These predictive models need to be deployed in the production environment of the company, so they can be used in the development of artificial intelligence based applications. The aim of this data science lifecycle is high speed delivery and completion of data science projects toward a defined engagement end point. Seamless execution of any data science project requires effective communication of tasks within the team as well as to the stakeholders.

The fundamental components of the "Team Data Science Process" are:

Definition of a data science lifecycle

The five major stages of the TDSP lifecycle that outline the interactive steps required for project execution from start to finish are: "Business understanding", "Data acquisition in understanding", "modeling", "deployment" and "customer acceptance". Keep reading for details on this to come shortly!

Standardized project structure

To enable seamless and easy access to project documents for the team members allowing for quick retrieval of information, use of templates, and a shared directory structure goes a long way. All project documents and the project code our store and a "version control system" such as "TFS", "Git", or "Subversion" for improved team collaboration. Business requirements and associated tasks and functionalities are stored in an agile project tracking system like "JIRA", "Rally", and "Azure DevOps" to enable enhanced tracking of code for every single functionality. These tools also help in the estimation of resources and costs involved through the project lifecycle. To ensure effective management of each project, information security and team collaboration, TDSP confers the creation of separate storage for each project on the version control system. The adoption of a standardized structure for all the projects within an organization aid in the creation of an institutional knowledge library across the organization.

The TDSP lifecycle provides standard templates for all the required documents as well as folder structure at a centralized location. The files containing programming codes for the data exploration and extraction of the functionality can be organized to using the provided a folder structure, which also holds records pertaining to model iterations. These templates allow the team members to easily understand the work that has been completed by others as well as for a seamless addition of new team members to a given project. The markdown format supports ease of accessibility as well as making edits or updates to the document templates. To make sure the project goal and objectives are well defined and also to ensure the expected quality of the deliverables, these templates provide various checklists with important questions for each project. For example, a "project charter" can be used to document the project scope and the business problem that is being resolved by the project; standardized data reports are used to document the "structure and statistics" of the data.

Infrastructure and resources for data science projects

To effectively store infrastructure and manage shared analytics, the TDSP recommends using tools like: "machine learning service", databases, "big data clusters", and cloud based systems to store data sets. The analytics and storage infrastructure that houses raw as well as processed or cleaned data sets can be cloud-based or on-premises. D analytics and storage infrastructure permits the reproducibility of analysis and prevents duplication and the redundancy of data that can create inconsistency and unwarranted infrastructure costs. Tools are supplied to grant specific permissions to the shared resources and to track their activity which in turn allows secure access to the resources for each member of the team.

Tools and utilities for project execution

The introduction of any changes to an existing process tends to be rather challenging in most organizations. To encourage and raise the consistency of adoption of these changes, several tools can be implemented that are provided by the TDSP. Some of the basic tasks in the data science lifecycle including "data exploration" and "baseline modeling" can be easily automated with the tools provided by TDSP. To allow hassle free contribution of shared tools and utilities into the team's "shared code repository", TDSP from provides a well defined structure. This results in cost savings by allowing other project teams within the organization to reuse and repurpose these shared tools and utilities.

The TDSP lifecycle serves as a standardized template with a well-defined set of artifacts that can be used to garner effective team collaboration and communication across the board. This lifecycle is comprised of a selection of the best practices and structures from "Microsoft" to facilitated successful delivery predictive analytics Solutions and intelligent applications.

Let's look at the details of each of the five stages of the TDSP lifecycle, namely, "Business understanding", "Data acquisition in understanding", "modeling", "deployment" and "customer acceptance".

Data Science Lifecycle

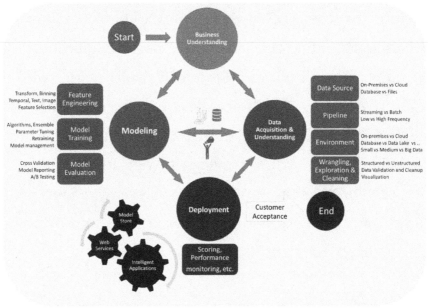

Stage I – Business understanding

The goal of this stage is to gather and drill down on the essential variables that will be used as targets for the model, and the metrics associated with these variables will ultimately determine the overall success of the project. Another significant objective of this stage is the identification of required data sources that the company already has or may need to procure. At this stage, the two primary tasks that are required to be accomplished are: "defining objects and identifying data sources".

Defining objectives

All projects must always start with the identification of the key business variables that the analytical tools are required to predict. These variables are called "model targets", and the metrics associated with these model targets such as sales forecast and prediction of fraudulent orders, are used as a measure of the success of the project. To define the project goals and objectives, it is imperative to work with the stakeholders and the end users and asking relevant questions that can be highly specific or even vague. To answer these questions, the data science approach employs names and numbers. The five types of questions that are primarily used for data science or machine learning are pertaining to: "regression (how much or how many?), classification (what categories?), clustering (which groups?), anomaly detection (is this unusual?), recommendation (which option should be taken?)". It is important to determine the right questions for your project and understand how the answers to these questions will help you accomplish the business or project goals.

Specification and alignment of the roles and responsibilities of each member within the project team is quintessential to the success of the project. This can be accomplished with the help of a high level project plan containing significant milestones that can be modified as needed to the course of the project. Another important definition that should be agreed upon at this stage of the project is that all of the key performance indicators and metrics. For example, a project for prediction of customer turnover rate requiring the accuracy rate of "ABC" percent by the completion of the project can help you understand the requirement that must be fulfilled to meet the success criteria of the project. So in order to achieve the "ABC" percent accuracy rate, the company may run discount offers and promotions. The industry wide standard used in the development of metrics is called "SMART", which stands for "Specific, Measurable, Achievable, Relevant, Time bound".

Identification of data sources

The data sources that may contain "known examples" of answers to the five types of questions raised during the defining phase must be identified and accounted for. You must look for data that is in direct relevance to the questions asked and assess if you have a measurable target and features related to those targets. The data that serves as an accurate measure for the model target and its features is crucial for the determination of the project's success. For example, you might encounter a situation where the existing system is unable to collect and record the types of data that are required to accomplish the project goals. This should immediately inform you that you need to start looking for external data sources or run a system update to enable the collection of additional data types by the existing system.

Deliverables to be created in this stage

- **Charter document** – It is a "living document" that needs to be updated throughout the course of the project, in light of new project discoveries and changing business requirements. A standard template is supplied with the TDSP "project structure definition". It is important to build up on this document by adding more details throughout the course of the project while keeping the stakeholders promptly updated on all changes made.
- **Data sources** – Within the TDSP "project data report folder", the data sources can be found within the "Raw Data Sources" section of the "Data

Definitions Report". The "Raw Data Sources" section also specifies the initial and final locations of the raw data and provide additional details like the "coding scripts" to move up the data to any desired environment.

- **Data dictionaries** – The descriptions of the characteristics and features of the data such as the "data schematics" and available "entity relationship diagrams", provided by the stakeholders are documented within the Data dictionaries.

Stage II – Data acquisition and understanding

The goal of this stage is the production of high quality processed data set with defined relationships to the model targets and location of the data set in the required analytics environment. At this stage, the "solution architecture" of the data pipeline must also be developed which will allow regular updates to and scoring of the data. The three primary tasks that must be completed during this stage are: "Data ingestion, Data exploration and Data pipeline set up".

Data ingestion

The process required to transfer the data from the source location to the target location should be set up in this phase. The target locations are determined by the environments that will allow you to perform analytical activities like training and predictions.

Data exploration

The data set must be scrubbed to remove any discrepancies and errors before it can be used to train the Data models. To check the data quality and gathered information required to process the data before modeling, tools such as data summarization and visualization should be used. Since this process is repeated multiple times, an automated utility called "IDEAR", which is provided by TDSP can be used for Data visualization and creation of Data summary reports. With the achievement of satisfactory quality of the processed data, the inherent data patterns can be observed. This, in turn, helps in the selection and development of an appropriate "predictive model" for the target. Now you must assess if you have the required amount of data to start the modeling process, which is iterative in nature and may require you to identify new data sources to achieve higher relevance and accuracy.

Set up a data pipeline

To supplement the iterative process of data modeling, a standard process for scoring new data and refreshing the existing data set must be established by setting up a "data pipeline or workflow". The solution architecture of the data pipeline must be developed by the end of this stage. There are three types of pipelines that can be used on the basis of the business needs and constraints of the existing system: "batch based", "real-time or streaming", and "hybrid".

Deliverables to be created in this stage

- **Data quality report** – This report must include a "data summary" relationship between the business requirement and its attributes and variable ranking among other details. The "IDEAR" tool supplied with TDSP it's capable of generating data quality reports on a relational table, CSV file or any other tabular data set.

- **Solution architecture** – A description or a diagram of the data pipeline that is used to score new data and generated predictions, after the model has been built can be referred to as "solution architecture". This diagram can also provide the data pipeline needed to "retrain" the model based on new data.

- **Checkpoint decision** –Prior to that start of the actual model building process project must be reevaluated to determine if the expected value can be achieved by pursuing the project. These are also called "Go or No-Go" decisions.

Stage III – Modeling

The goal of this stage is to find "optimal data features" for the machine learning model, which is informative enough to predict the target variables accurately and can be deployed in the production environment. The three primary tasks that must be accomplished in this stage are: "feature engineering, model training, and the determination of the suitability of the model for the production environment".

Feature engineering

The data features must be created from the raw data variables using the process of "inclusion, aggregation, and transformation". To be able to understand the functioning of the model, a clear understanding of how these data features relate to one another as well as to the machine learning algorithms that will be using those features must be developed. The insights gathered from the data exploration phase can be combined with the domain expertise to allow creative feature engineering. The fine act of determining and including informative variables while making sure a whole lot of unrelated variables are not included in the data set is referred to as feature engineering. Too many unrelated variables will add noise to the data model, so an attempt must be made to add as many informative variables as possible to get better results. The features must also be generated for any new data collected doing the scoring.

Model training

A wide variety of modeling algorithms are available in the market today. The algorithm that meets the criteria of your project must be selected. The process for "model training" can be divided into four steps which are:

1. Creation of a "training data set" as well as a "test data set" by appropriately dividing the input data.

2. Development of the model with the use of the "training data set".

3. Evaluation of the training and the test data set, by employing various machine learning algorithms as well as related "tuning parameters" that are designed to help answer the previously discussed five types of questions from the existing data set.

4. Assess the best fit for the solution to resolve the business problem by comparing all available methods using key performance indicators and metrics.

TDSP provides an "automated modeling and reporting tool" that is capable of running through multiple algorithms and "parameters sweeps" to develop a "baseline model" as well as a "baseline modeling report" that can serve as a performance summary for each "model and parameter combination".

Deliverables to be created in this stage

- **Feature sets** – The document containing all the features described in the "feature sets section of the data definition report". It is heavily used by the programmers to write the required code and develop features based on the basis of the description provided by the document.

- **Model report** – This document must contain the details of each model that was evaluated based on a standard template report.
- **Checkpoint decisions** – A decision regarding deployment of the model to the production environment must be made on the basis of the performance of different models.

Stage IV – Deployment

The goal of this stage is to release the solution models to a lower production like environment such as a pre-production environment and user acceptance testing environment before eventually deploying the model in the production environment. The primary task to be accomplished in this stage is the "operationalization of the model".

Operationalize the model

Once you have obtained a set of models with expected performance levels, these models can then be operationalized for other applicable applications to use.

According to the business requirements, predictions can be made in real-time or on a batch basis. In order to deploy the model, they must be integrated with an open "Application Programming Interface" (API) to allow interaction of the model with all other applications and its components, as needed.

Deliverables to be created in this stage

- A dashboard report using the key performance indicators and metrics to access the health of the system.
- A document or run book with the details of the deployment plan for the final model.
- A document containing the solution architecture of the final model.

Stage V – Customer Acceptance

The goal of this stage is to ensure that the final solution for the project meets the expectations of the stakeholders and fulfills the business requirements gathered during Stage I of the Data science lifecycle. The two primary tasks that must be accomplished in this stage are: "system validation and project hand-off".

System validation – The final solution that will be deployed in the production environment must be evaluated against the business requirements and the data pipeline to make sure that the stakeholders needs are met. The stakeholder must validate that the system meets their business needs and resolves the problem that started the project in the first place. All the documentation must be thoroughly reviewed and finalized by the end of this stage.

Project hand-off – At this stage, the project must be transferred from the development team to the post production and maintenance team. For example, the IT support team or someone from the stakeholder's team dad will provide day-to-day support for the solution in the production environment.

Deliverables to be created in this stage

The most important document created during this stage is for the stakeholders and called an "exit report". The document contains all of the available details of the project that are significant to provide an understanding of the operations of the system. TDSP supplies a standardized template for the "exit report", that can be easily customized to cater to specific stakeholder needs.

Review Quiz

Answer the questions below to verify your understanding of the concepts explained in this chapter. The answer key can be found at the end of the quiz.

1. What are the 5 different stages of a data science lifecycle.

2. Name any 2 deliverables that need to be created at the end of the first stage of the lifecycle.

3. Data ingestion and exploration are performed at which stage of the lifecycle?

4. Feature sets, model reports, and checkpoint decisions are created as deliverables at the end of ____ stage of the data science lifecycle.

5. In order to deploy the model, they must be integrated with an open ____ to allow interaction of the model with all other applications and its components.

Answer Key

1. Business Understanding, Data acquisition, and understanding, Modeling, Deployment, Customer acceptance

2. Charter document, Data sources, Data dictionaries

3. Data acquisition and understanding

4. Modeling

5. Application Programming Interface or API

Day 3: Big Data 101

Big Data

In 2001, Gartner defined Big data as "Data that contains greater variety arriving in increasing volumes and with ever-higher velocity". This led to the formulation of the "three V's". Big data refers to an avalanche of structured and unstructured data that is endlessly flooding and from a variety of endless data sources. These data sets are too large to be analyzed with traditional analytical tools and technologies but have a plethora of valuable insights hiding underneath.

The "Vs" of Big data

Volume – To be classified as big data, the volume of the given data set must be substantially larger than traditional data sets. These data sets are primarily composed of unstructured data with limited structured and semi-structured data. The unstructured data or the data with unknown value can be collected from input sources such as webpages, search history, mobile applications, and social media platforms. The size and customer base of the company is usually proportional to the volume of the data acquired by the company.

Velocity – The speed at which data can be gathered and acted upon the first to the velocity of big data. Companies are increasingly using a combination of on-premise and cloud-based servers to increase the speed of their data collection. The modern-day "Smart Products and Devices" require real-time access to consumer data, in order to be able to provide them a more engaging and enhanced user experience.

Variety – Traditionally a data set would contain majority of structured data with low volume of unstructured and semi-structured data, but the advent of big data has given rise to new unstructured data types such as video, text, audio that require sophisticated tools and technologies to clean and process these data types to extract meaningful insights from them.

Veracity – Another "V" that must be considered for big data analysis is veracity. This refers to the "trustworthiness or the quality" of the data. For example, social media platforms like "Facebook" and "Twitter" with blogs and posts containing a hashtag, acronyms, and all kinds of typing errors can significantly reduce the reliability and accuracy of the data sets.

Value – Data has evolved as a currency of its own with intrinsic value. Just like traditional monetary currencies, the ultimate value of the big data is directly proportional to the insight gathered from it.

History of Big Data

The origin of large volumes of data can be traced back to the 1960s and 1970s when the Third Industrial Revolution had just started to kick in, and the development of relational databases had begun along with the construction of data centers. But the concept of big data has recently taken center stage primarily since the availability of free search engines like Google and Yahoo, free online entertainment services like YouTube and social media platforms like Facebook. In 2005, businesses started to recognize the incredible amount of user data being generated through these platforms and services and in the same year and open-source framework called "Hadoop", was developed to gather and analyze these large data dumps available to the companies. During the same period, a non-relational or distributed database called "NoSQL" started to gain popularity due to its ability to store and extract unstructured data. "Hadoop" made it possible for the companies to work with big data with high ease and at a relatively low cost.

Today with the rise of cutting edge technology not only humans but machines also generating data. The smart device technologies like "Internet of things" (IoT) and "Internet of systems" (IoS) have skyrocketed the volume of big data. Our everyday household objects and smart devices are connected to the Internet and able to track and record our usage patterns as well as our interactions with these products and feeds all this data directly into the big data. The advent of machine learning technology has further increased the volume of data generated on a daily basis. It is estimated that by 2020, "1.7 MB of data will be generated per second per person". As the big data will continue to grow, its usability still has many horizons to cross.

Importance of big data

To gain reliable and trustworthy information from a data set, it is very important to have a complete data set that has been made possible with the use of big data technology. The more data we have, the more information and details can be extracted out of it. To gain a 360 view of a problem and its underlying solutions, the future of big data is very promising. Here are some examples of the use of big data:

Product development – Large and small e-commerce businesses are increasingly relying upon big data to understand customer demands and expectations. Companies can develop predictive models to launch new products and services by using primary characteristics of their past and existing products and services and generating a model describing the relationship of those characteristics with the commercial success of those products and services. For example, a leading fast manufacturing commercial goods company, "Procter & Gamble", extensively uses big data gathered from the social media websites, test markets, and focus groups in preparation for their new product launch.

Predictive maintenance – In order to besides leave project potential mechanical and equipment failures, a large volume of unstructured data such as error messages, log entries and normal temperature of the machine must be analyzed along with available structured data such as make and model of the equipment and year of manufacturing. By analyzing this big data set using the required analytical tools, companies can extend the shelf life of their equipment by preparing for scheduled maintenance ahead of time and predicting future occurrences of potential mechanical failures.

Customer experience – The smart customer is aware of all of the technological advancements and is loyal only to the most engaging and enhanced user experience available. This has triggered a race among the companies to provide unique customer experiences analyzing the data gathered from customers' interactions with the company's products and services. Providing personalized recommendations and offers to reduce customer churn rate and effectively kind words prospective leads into paying customers.

Fraud and compliance – Big data helps in identifying the data patterns and assessing historical trends from previous fraudulent transactions to effectively detect and prevent potentially fraudulent transactions. Banks, financial institutions, and online payment services like "PayPal" are constantly monitoring and gathering customer transaction data in an effort to prevent fraud.

Operational efficiency – With the help of big data predictive analysis. companies can learn and anticipate future demand and product trends by analyzing production capacity, customer feedback, and data pertaining to top-selling items and product returns to improve decision-making and produce products that are in line with the current market trends.

Machine learning – For a machine to be able to learn and train on its own, it requires a humongous volume of data i.e. big data. A solid training set containing structured, semi-structured and unstructured data, will help the machine to develop a multidimensional view of the real world and the problem it is engineered to resolve.

Drive innovation – By studying and understanding the relationships between humans and their electronic devices as well as the manufacturers of these devices, companies can develop improved and innovative products by examining current product trends and meeting customer expectations.

"The importance of big data doesn't revolve around how much data you have, but what you do with it. You can take data from any source and analyze it to find answers that enable 1) cost reductions, 2) time reductions, 3) new product development and optimized offerings, and 4) smart decision making".

- SAS

The functioning of big data

There are three important actions required to gain insights from big data:

Integration – The traditional data integration methods such as ETL (Extract, Transform, Load) are incapable of collating data from a wide variety of unrelated sources and applications that are you at the heart of big data. Advanced tools and technologies are required to analyze big data sets that are exponentially larger than traditional data sets. By integrating big data from these disparate sources, companies are able to analyze and extract valuable insight to grow and maintain their businesses.

Management – Big data management can be defined as "the organization, administration, and governance of large volumes of both structured and unstructured data". Big data requires efficient and cheap storage, which can be accomplished using servers that are on-premises, cloud-based or a combination of both. Companies are able to seamlessly access required data from anywhere across the world and then processing this is a data using required processing engines on an as-needed basis. The goal is to make sure the quality of the data is high-level and can be accessed easily by the required tools and applications. Big data gathered from all kinds of Dale sources including social media platforms, search engine history and call logs. The big data usually contain large sets of unstructured data and the semi-structured data which are stored in a variety of formats. To be able to process and store this complicated data, companies require more powerful and advanced data management software beyond the traditional relational databases and data warehouse platforms. New platforms are available in the market that is capable of combining big data with the traditional data warehouse systems in a "logical data warehousing architecture". As part of this effort, companies are required to make decisions on what data must be secured for regulatory purposes and compliance, what data must be kept for future analytical purposes and what data has no future use and can be disposed of. This process is called "data classification", which allows a rapid and efficient analysis of a subset of data to be included in the immediate decision-making process of the company.

Analysis – Once the big data has been collected and is easily accessible, it can be analyzed using advanced analytical tools and technologies. This analysis will provide valuable insight and actionable information. Big data can be explored to make discoveries and develop data models using artificial intelligence and machine learning algorithms.

Big Data Analytics

The terms of big data and big data analytics are often used interchangeably owing to the fact that the inherent purpose of big data is to be analyzed. "Big data analytics" can be defined as a set of qualitative and quantitative methods that can be employed to examine a large amount of unstructured, structured, and semi-structured data to discover data patterns and valuable hidden insights. Big data analytics is the science of analyzing big data to collect metrics, key performance indicators and Data trends that can be easily lost in the flood of raw data, buy using machine learning algorithms and automated analytical techniques. The different steps involved in "big data analysis" are:

Gathering Data Requirements – It is important to understand what information or data needs to be gathered to meet the business objective and goals. Data organization is also very critical for efficient and accurate data analysis. Some of the categories in which the data can be organized are gender, age, demographics, location, ethnicity, and income. A decision must also be made on the required data types (qualitative and quantitative) and data values (can be numerical or alphanumerical) to be used for the analysis.

Gathering Data – Raw data can be collected from disparate sources such as social media platforms, computers, cameras, other software applications, company websites, and even third-party data providers. The big data analysis inherently requires large volumes of data, the majority of which is unstructured with a limited amount of structured and semi-structured data.

Data organization and categorization – Depending on the company's infrastructure Data organization could be done on a simple Excel spreadsheet or using and man tools and applications that are capable of processing statistical data. Data must be organized and categorized based on data requirements collected in step one of the big data analysis process.

Cleaning the data – to perform the big data analysis sufficiently and rapidly, it is very important to make sure the data set is void of any redundancy and errors. Only a complete data set fulfilling the Data requirements must have proceeded to the final analysis step. Preprocessing of data is required to make sure the only high-quality data is being analyzed and company resources are being put to good use.

"Big data is high-volume, and high-velocity and/or high-variety information assets that demand cost-effective, innovative forms of information processing that enable enhanced insight, decision making, and process automation".

- Gartner

Analyzing the data – Depending on the insight that is expected to be achieved by the completion of the analysis, any of the following four different types of big data analytics approach can be adopted:

- **Predictive analysis** – This type of analysis is done to generate forecasts and predictions for future plans of the company. By the completion of predictive analysis of the company's big data, the future state of the company can be more precisely predicted and derived from the current state of the company. The business executives are keenly interested in this analysis to make sure the company day-to-day operations are in line with the future vision of the company. For example, to deploy advanced analytical tools and applications in the sales division of a company, the first step is to analyze the leading source of data. Once believes source analysis has been completed the type and number of communication channels for the sales team must be analyzed. This is followed by the use of machine learning algorithms on customer data to gain insight into how the existing customer base is interacting with the company's products or services. This predictive analysis will conclude with the deployment of artificial intelligence based tools to skyrocket the company's sales.

- **Prescriptive analysis** – Analysis that is carried out by primarily focusing on the business rules and recommendations to generate a selective analytical path as prescribed by the industry standards to boost company performance. The goal of this analysis is to understand the intricacies of various departments of the organization and what measures should be taken by the company to be able to gain insights from its customer data by using a prescribed analytical pathway. This allows the company to embrace domain specificity and conciseness by providing a sharp focus on it's existing and future big data analytics process.

- **Descriptive analysis** – All the incoming data received and stored by the company can be analyzed to produce insightful descriptions on the basis of the results obtained. The goal of this analysis is to identify data patterns and current market trends that can be adopted by the company to grow its business. For example, credit card companies often require risk assessment results on all prospective customers to be able to make predictions on the likelihood of the customer failing to make their credit payments and make a decision whether the customer should be approved for the credit or not. This risk assessment it's primarily based on the customer's credit history but also takes into account other influencing factors including remarks from other financial institutions that the customer had approached for credit, customer income and financial performance as well as their digital footprint and social media profile.

- **Diagnostic analysis** – As the name suggests, this type of analysis is done to "diagnose" or understand why a certain event unfolded and how that event can be prevented from occurring in the future or replicated if needed. For example, web marketing strategies and campaigns often employ social media platforms to get publicity and increase their goodwill. Not all campaigns are as successful as expected; therefore, learning from failed campaigns is just as important if not more. Companies can run diagnostic analysis on their campaign by collecting data pertaining to the "social media mentions" of the campaign, number of campaign page views, the average amount of time spent on the campaign page by an individual, number of social media fans and followers of the campaign, online reviews and other related metrics to understand why the campaign failed and how future campaigns can be made more effective.

The big data analysis can be conducted using one or more of the tools listed below:

- Hadoop – Open source data framework.
- Python – Programming language widely used for machine learning.
- SAS – Advanced analytical tool used primarily for big data analysis.

- Tableau – Artificial intelligence based tool used primarily for data visualization.

- SQL – the Programming language used to extract data from relational databases.

- Splunk – Analytical tool used to categorize machine-generated data

- R-programming – the Programming language used primarily for statistical computing.

Applications of Big Data Analytics

The big data analytics is involved in every business centralize on quick and agile decisions to stay competitive. Some of the different types of organizations that can use big data analytics are:

Education industry

Big data has allowed customization of learning programs according to individual student's needs and learning capabilities to accelerate their academic growth. Real time monitoring and analysis of student's classroom interactions can be used to enhance study course material. With the help of big data analysis, standardized testing has been upgraded to account for student learning curves.

Healthcare

The amount of data generated in healthcare is skyrocketing. Digital patient records, health insurance provider information, various health plans offered by the employers, and other pertinent information constitutes big data and can be very tedious to manage. With the advent of big data analytics, healthcare providers can uncover valuable insights from this data and use those insights to develop life saving diagnostic tools and treatment options and a much shorter period in comparison to following a standard protocol. Hospital equipment, patient entry and exit, course of treatment administered and other related activities can be effectively tracked in real-time and optimized to provide better patient care. It is estimated that around $63 billion can be saved in global healthcare costs by simply making the healthcare system only 1% more efficient, using big data analysis.

Travel Industry

Social media platforms often serve as a diary of our digital lives with easily accessible data generated by the users that can be analyzed by the company to uncover hidden data trends and extracting valuable insight into customer expectations and preferences. The travel industry, including Hotels and airlines, uses big data analytics to understand how customers are interacting with the company's products and services. These companies are always looking for ways to pump up their bottom line by increasing the conversion rate of a prospective customer into a paying consumer. By understanding individual customers, companies can predict their future travel plans and try to lure them into staying with the company my offering personalized travel packages and discounts.

Finance

It is very important for financial institutions and banks to be very agile and nimble with their decision making process as they adjust to the fluctuating economy. With the help of powerful big data analytical tools, companies can extract valuable insight from the data at a rapid pace, so as to be included in the immediate decision making process. By eliminating overlapping and redundant tools and systems, companies can save a lot of money on overhead costs increase their operational efficiency. Having the required information available immediately allows banks and financial institutions to provide excellent customer service.

Manufacturing

Product manufacturers are frequently encountering complex supply chain management issues as well as equipment breakdown and failure issues. In the manufacturing industry, companies are able to predict potential equipment failure in the near future and plan equipment maintenance ahead of time to avail maximum equipment shelf life and efficiency. By gathering and analyzing all of the supply chain data pertaining to the company's line of products, using advanced analytical tools and algorithms, companies can identify the optimal logistics pathway for their products as well as third party providers that can potentially result in cost savings. Companies can also gather insights on new cost-saving opportunities and areas of expansion that could have been easily missed in a large volume of data.

Retail

The smart customer of today has high expectations from retailers to accurately understand customer demand and provide products and services that are in line with those expectations. Companies are required to have a sound understanding of what the customer wants, how the product should be marketed and the best time to launch a product dictated by the current market trends. The customer insights needed to accomplish this goal can only be gathered using the big data analytics on all available consumer data collected from a wide variety of sources such as consumer persona, purchase history, customer loyalty programs, social media activities, customer interaction with the company websites and other related data sources. Every company has its own customer database and depending on the analytical tools and algorithms applied to their big data and the information sought after, they can easily lead the competition by increasing customer loyalty and achieving a high conversion rate of prospective customers into paying consumers.

For companies like Amazon, Facebook, and Google the big data analytical tools make up the most important weapons in their arsenal. These digital first Enterprises cannot survive. Amazon is the leader of highly customized and personalized expedience being offered to the consumers. Amazon has widely deployed big data analytics to make use of all available data to build and hands customer profiles and offer them product recommendations based on their order history among other contributing factors. The humongous amount of data that is available to Google is unimaginable. Thanks to billions of searches carried on the Google search engine; the company has evolved as one of the most data intensive companies in the world. This motherload of data requires big data analytical tools to provide valuable insights to Google that can in turn, further enhance and improve our digital lives. Facebook is contemplating the use of big data analytics to gain insight into what their users are talking about so as to understand what products and services they would be interested in. The free Facebook platform makes money from the millions of advertisements sponsored by big and small businesses so it's critical for the company to understand the pulse of its users and make sure the advertisements that are displayed on the site our current and customized to meet every user's expectations.

Life sciences - The field of clinical research is a highly capital-intensive and extremely slow process with trials feeling for a variety of reasons. The artificial intelligence and the Internet of medical things technology have opened up new horizons for improving speed and efficiency at every stage of clinical research by providing more intelligent and automated Solutions.

Big Data Analysis Vs. Data Visualization

In the wider data community, data analysis and data visualization are increasingly being used synonymously. Professional data analysts are expected to be able to skillfully represent data using visual tools and formats. On the other hand, new professional job positions called "Data visualization expert" and "data artist" have hit the market. But companies stool need professionals to analyze their data and extract valuable insights from it. As you have learned by now, Data analysis or big data analysis is an "exploratory process" with defined goals and specific questions that need to be answered from a given set of big data. Data visualization pertains to the visual representation of data, using tools as simple as an Excel spreadsheet or as advanced as dashboards created using Tableau. Business executives are always short on time and need to capture a whole lot of details. Therefore, the data analyst is required to use effective visualizations that can significantly lower the amount of time needed to understand the presented data and gather valuable insights from the data. By developing a variety of visual presentations from the data, an analyst can view the data from different perspectives and identify potential data trends, outliers, gaps, and anything that stands out and warrants further analysis. This process is referred to as "visual analytics". Some of the widely used visual representations of the data are "dashboard reports", "infographics", and "data story". These visual representations are considered as the final deliverable from the big data analysis process but in reality, they frequently serve as a starting point for future political activities. The two completely different activities of data visualization and big data analysis are inherently related and loop into each other by serving as a starting point for as well as the endpoint of the other activity.

Review Quiz

Answer the questions below to verify your understanding of the concepts explained in this chapter. The answer key can be found at the end of the quiz.

1. Name the Vs of the Big data.
2. Define Big Data Analytics.

3. What are the two smart technologies significantly contributing to the increasing volume of data?

4. As of 2020, how much data will be produced by human digital activity?

5. What are the three important actions required to gain insights from big data?

6. What type of analysis is used to understand why a certain event unfolded and how that event can be prevented from occurring in the future or replicated?

7. What is the difference between data analysis and data visualization?

Answer Key

1. Volume, Velocity, Variety, Veracity, Value

2. A set of qualitative and quantitative methods that can be employed to examine a large amount of unstructured, structured and semi structured data to discover data patterns and valuable hidden insights.

3. Internet of Things, Internet of Systems

4. 1.7 MB per person per second

5. Integration, Management, and Analysis

6. Diagnostic Analysis

7. Data analysis or big data analysis is an exploratory process with defined goals and specific questions that need to be answered from a given set of big data. Data visualization pertains to the visual representation of data, using tools as simple as an Excel spreadsheet or as advanced as dashboards.

Day 4: Basics of Data Mining

Data mining can be defined as "the process of exploring and analyzing large volumes of data to gather meaningful patterns and rules". Data mining falls under the umbrella of data science and is heavily used to build artificial intelligence based machine learning models, for example, search engine algorithms. Although the process of "digging through data" to uncover hidden patterns and predict future events has been around for a long time and referred to as "knowledge discovery in databases", the term "Data mining" was coined as recently as the 1990s. Data mining consists of three foundational and highly intertwined disciplines of science, namely, "statistics" (the mathematical study of data relationships), "machine learning algorithms" (algorithms that can be trained with an inherent capability to learn) and "artificial intelligence" (machines that can display human-like intelligence). With the advent of big data, Data mining technology has been evolved to keep up with the "limitless potential of big data" and affordable computing power. The once considered tedious, labor-intensive and time consuming activities have been automated using advance processing speed and power of the modern computing systems.

"Data mining is the process of finding anomalies, patterns, and correlations within large data sets to predict outcomes. Using a broad range of techniques, you can use this information to increase revenues, cut costs, improve customer relationships, reduce risks and more".

– SAS

According to SAS, "unstructured data alone makes up 90% of the digital universe". This avalanche of big data does not necessarily guarantee more knowledge. The application of data mining technology allows the filtering of all the redundant and unnecessary data noise to garner the understanding of relevant information that can be used in the immediate decision-making process.

Applications of data mining

The applications of data mining technology are far and wide, ranging from retail pricing and promotions to credit risk assessment by financial institutions and banks. Every industrial sector is benefiting from the applications the data mining technology.

Here are some of the examples of industrial applications and data mind technology:

Healthcare bio-informatics

To predict the likelihood of the patient suffering from one or more health conditions given the risk factors, statistical models are used by healthcare professionals. Genetically transferred diseases can be prevented or mediated from the onset of deteriorating health conditions, by modeling the patient's genetic, family and demographic data. In developing nations, there is a scarcity of healthcare professionals. Therefore, assisted diagnoses and prioritization of patients is very critical. Data mining based models have recently been deployed in such countries to help with the prioritization of patients before healthcare professionals can reach these countries and administer treatment.

Credit risk management

Financial institutions and banks deploy data mining models tools to predict the likelihood of a potential credit card customer failing to make their credit payments on time as well as to determine appropriate credit limit that the customer may qualify for. These data mining models collect and extract information from a variety of input sources including personal information, Financial history of the customer at and demographic among other sources. The model then provides the institution or bank interest rate to be collected from the client based on the assessed risk. For example, Data mining models take the credit score of the applicant into consideration and individuals with a low Credit score are given the high interest rates.

Spam filtering

A lot of email clients such as "Google mail" and "Yahoo mail" rely on the data mining tools to detect and flag email spam and malware. By analyzing hundreds and thousands of shared characteristics of spams and malware, the data mining tool provides insight that can be used in the development of enhanced security measures and tools. These applications are not only capable of detecting spam, but they are also very efficient in categorizing the spam emails and storing them in a separate folder, so they never enter the user's inbox.

Marketing

Retail companies have an incessant need to understand their customer demands and expectations. With the use of data mining tools, businesses can analyze customer related data such as purchase history, demographics, gender and age to gather valuable customer insights and segment them into groups based on shared shopping attributes. Companies then devise unique marketing strategies and campaigns to target specific groups such as discount offers and promotions.

Sentiment analysis

With the use of a technique called "text mining", companies can analyze their data from all of their social media platforms to understand the "sentiment" of their customer base.

This process of understanding the feelings of a big group of people towards a particular topic is called "sentiment analysis" and can be carried out using data mining tools. With the use of pattern recognition technology, input data from social media platforms and other related public content websites are collected using the "text mining" technology and identify data patterns that feed into a general understanding of the topic. To further dive into this data, the "natural language processing" technique can be used to understand the human language in a specific context.

Qualitative data mining

The "text mining" technique can also be used to perform quantitative research and gain insight from large volumes of unstructured data. Recently a research study conducted by the University of Berkeley revealed the use of data mining models and child welfare program studies.

Product recommendation systems

Advance "recommendations systems" are like the bread and butter for online retailers. The use of predictive customer behavior analysis is rising among small and large online businesses to gain a competitive edge in the market. Some of the largest e-commerce businesses including" Amazon", Macy's", and" Nordstrom", have invested millions of dollars in the development of their own proprietary data mining models to forecast market trends and all for a more engaging in enhanced user experience to their customers. The on-demand entertainment giant

"Netflix" bought over a million dollars worth algorithm to enhance the accuracy of their video recommendation system, which reportedly increased the recommendation accuracy for "Netflix" by over 8%.

The data mining process

Most widely used data mining processes can be broken down into six steps as listed below:

1. Business understanding

It is very critical to understand the project goals and what is it that you're trying to achieve through the data mining process. Companies always start with the establishment of a defined goal and a project plan that includes details such as individual team member roles and responsibility, project milestones, project timelines and key performance indicators and metrics.

2. Data understanding

Data is available from a wide variety of input sources and in different formats. With the use of data visualization tools, the data properties and features can be assessed to ensure the existing data set is able to meet the established business requirements and project goals.

3. Data preparation

The preprocessing of Data collected in multiple formats is very important. The data set must be scrubbed to remove data redundancies and identify gaps before it is deemed appropriate for mining. Considering the amount of data to be analyzed, the data pre-processing and processing steps can take a long time. To enhance the speed of the data mining process, instead of using a single system companies prefer using distributed systems as part of their "database management systems". The distributed systems also provide enhanced security measures by segregating the data into multiple devices rather than a single data warehouse. At this stage, it is also very crucial to account for backup options and failsafe measures in the event of data loss during the data manipulation stage.

4. Data modeling

Applicable mathematical models and analytical tools are applied to the data set to identify patterns.

5. Evaluation

The modeling results and data patterns are evaluating against the project goal and objectives to determine if the data findings can be released for use across the organization.

6. Deployment

Once the insights gathered from the data have been evaluated as applicable to the functioning and operations of the organization, these insights can be shared across the company to be included in its day-to-day operations. With the use of a Business Intelligence tool, the data findings can be stored at a centralized location and accessed using the BI tool as needed.

Pros of data mining

Automated decision-making

With the use of data mining technology, businesses can seamlessly automate tedious manual tasks and analyze large volumes of data to gather insights for the routine and critical decision-making process. For example, financial lending institutions, banks and online payment services use data mining technology to detect potentially fraudulent transactions, verify user identity and ensure data privacy to protect their customers against identity theft. When a company's operational algorithms are working in coordination with the data mining models, a company can independently gather, analyze and take actions on data to improve and streamline their operational decision-making process.

Accurate prediction and forecasting

Project planning is fundamental to the success of any company. Managers and executives can leverage data mining technology to gather reliable forecasts and predictions on future market trends and include in their future planning process. For example, one of the leading retail company "Macy's" has implemented demand forecasting models to generate reliable demand forecasts for Mary is clothing categories at individual stores, in order to increase the efficiency of their supply chain by routing the forecasted inventory to each store and cater to the needs of the market more efficiently.

Cost reduction

With the help of data mining technologies companies can maximize the use of their resources by smarty allocating them across the business model. The use of data mining technology in planning, as well as an automated decision-making process, results in accurate forecasts leading to significant cost reductions. For example, a major airline company "Delta" implemented RFID chips inside their passengers checked in baggage and gathered baggage handling data that was analyzed using data mining technology to identify improvement opportunities in their process and minimizing the number of mishandled baggage. This not only resulted in a cost saving on the search and rerouting process of the lost baggage but also translated into higher customer satisfaction.

Customer insights

Companies across different industrial sectors have deployed Data mining models to gather valuable insights from existing customer data, which can be used to segment and target customers with similar shopping attributes using similar marketing strategies and campaigns. Customer personas can be created using data mining technology to provide a more engaging and personalized user experience to the customer. For example, "Disney" has recently invested over billion dollars in developing and deploying "Magic bands", offering the convenience and enhanced experience and Disney resorts. At the same time, these bands can be used to collect data on patron activities and interactions with different "Disney" products and services at the park to further enhance the "Disney experience".

"When [data mining and] predictive analytics are done right, the analyses aren't a means to a predictive end; rather, the desired predictions become a means to analytical insight and discovery. We do a better job of analyzing what we really need to analyze and predicting what we really want to predict".

– Harvard Business Review Insight Center Report

Challenges of data mining

1. Big data

Our digital life has inundated companies with large volumes of data, which is estimated to reach 1.7 MB per second per person by 2020. This exponential increase in volume and complexity of big data has presented challenges for the data mining technology. Companies are looking to expedite their decision-making process by swiftly and efficiently extracting and analyzing data to gain valuable insights from their data treasure trove. The ultimate goal of data mining technology is to overcome these challenges and unlock the true potential of data value. The "4Vs" of big data namely velocity, variety, volume and veracity, represent the four major challenges facing the data mining technology.

The skyrocketing "velocity" or speed at which new data is being generated poses a challenge of increasing storage requirements. The "variety" or different data types collected and stored require advance data mining capabilities to be able to simultaneously process a multitude of data formats. Data mining tools that are not equipped to process such highly variable big data provide low value, due to their inefficiency and analyzing unstructured and structured data together.

The large volume of big data is not only challenging for storage but it's even more challenging do identify correct data in a timely manner, owing to a massive reduction in the speed of the data mining tools and algorithms. To add on to this challenge, the data "veracity" denoting that all of the collected data is not accurate and can be incomplete or even biased. The data mining tools are struggling to deliver high-quality results in a timely manner by analyzing high quantity or big data.

2. Overloading models

Data models that describe the natural errors of the data set instead of the underlying patterns are often "over-fitted" or overloaded. These models tend to be highly complex and the choir, a large number of independent media, bowls to precisely predict a future event. Data volume and variety further increase the risk of overloading. A high number of variables tend to restrict the data model within the confines of the known sample data. On the other hand, an insufficient number of variables can compromise the relevance of the model. To obtain the required number of variables for the data mining models, to be able to strike a balance between the accuracy of the results and the prediction capabilities is one of the major challenges facing the data mining technology today.

3. Data privacy and security

To cater to the large volume of big data generated on a daily basis, companies are investing in cloud based storage servers along with its on premise servers. The cloud computing technology is relatively new in the market and the inherent nature of this service poses multiple security and privacy concerns. Data privacy and security is one of the biggest concerns of the Smart consumers who are willing to take their business to. The company that can promise them the security of their personal information and data. This requires organizations to evaluate their customer relationships and prioritize customer privacy over the development of policies that can potentially compromise customer data security.

4. Scaling costs

With the increasing speed of data generation leading to a high volume of complex data, organizations are required to expand their data mining models and deploy them across the organization. To unlock the full potential of data mining tools, companies are required to heavily invest in computing infrastructure and processing power to efficiently run the data mining models. Big ticket item purchase including data servers, software and advance computers, must be made in order to scale the analytical capabilities of the organization.

Data Mining Trends

Increased Computing Speed

With increasing volume and complexity of big data, Data mining tools need more powerful and faster computers to efficiently analyze data. The existing statistical techniques like "clustering" art equipment to process only thousands of input data with a limited number of variables. However, companies are gathering over millions of new data observations with hundreds of variables making the analysis too complicated for the computing system to process.

The big data is going to continue to explode, demanding super computers that are powerful enough to rapidly and efficiently analyze the growing big data.

Language standardization

The data science community is actively looking to standardize a language for the data mining process. This ongoing effort will allow the analyst to conveniently work with a variety of data mining platforms by mastering one standard Data mining language.

Scientific mining

The success of data mining technology in the industrial world has caught the eye of the scientific and academic research community. For example, psychologists are using "association analysis" to capture her and identify human behavioral patterns for research purposes. Economists are using protective analysis algorithms to forecast future market trends by analyzing current market variables.

Web mining

Web mining can be defined as "the process of discovering hidden data patterns and chains using similar techniques of data mining and applying them directly on the Internet". The three main types of web mining are: "content mining", "usage mining", and "structure mining". For example, "Amazon" uses web mining to gain an understanding of customer interactions with their website and mobile application, to provide more engaging and enhanced user experience to their customers.

Data mining tools

Some of the most widely used data mining tools are:

Orange

Orange is an "open source component-based software written in Python". It is most frequently used for basic data mining analysis and offers top-of-the-line data pre-processing features.

RapidMiner

RapidMiner is an "open source component-based software written in Java". It is most frequently used for "predictive analysis" and offers integrated environments for "machine learning", "deep learning", and "text mining".

Mahout

Mahout is an open source platform primarily used for unsupervised learning process" and developed by "Apache". It is most frequently used to develop "machine learning algorithms for clustering, classification and collaborative filtering". This software requires advanced knowledge and expertise to be able to leverage the full capabilities of the platform.

MicroStrategy

MicroStrategy is a "business intelligence and data analytics software that can complement all data mining models". This platform offers a variety of drivers and gateways to seamlessly connect with any enterprise resource and analyze complex big data by transforming it into accessible visualizations that can be easily shared across the organization.

Day 5: Data Analysis Frameworks

Ensemble Learning

It is the method of combining predictions generated by various machine learning algorithms to create predictions of higher accuracy than any of the contributing algorithms. Simply put, an ensemble model consists of multiple contributing models or algorithms to process the underlying data either by boosting or bagging.

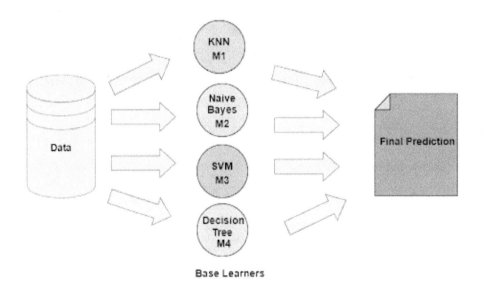

Base Learners

When a set of learning algorithms using weighted averages to transform weak models into strong learners is referred to as boosting. The preceding model will dictate the features that will be focused on and run by the subsequent model. The machine learning is boosted with repeated runs. On the other hand, bagging or bootstrap aggregation pertains to randomly selecting the data samples then replacing the data to achieve more accurate predictions. With this technique, the variance and bias of the dataset can be easily understood. This comes in handy when you are dealing with algorithms with high variance such as decision trees and need to decrease the variance of the model. Every model will process the dataset independently and aggregate the final output with no preference for any specific model.

Decision Trees

If you are thinking does this decision tree have any relation to the real life trees, then you are correct. A tree has few fundamental parts, primarily branches, leaves, trunk and roots. Similarly, a decision tree has multiple elements to help with the decision making process. A data science "decision tree" can be defined as a tree like graphical representation of the decision making process by taking into consideration all the conditions or factors that can influence the decision and the consequences of those decisions. Decision trees are considered one of the simplest "supervised machine learning algorithms" and has three main elements: "branch nodes" representing conditions, "edges" representing ongoing decision process and "leaf nodes" representing the end of the decision.

There are two types of decision trees: "Classification tree" that is used to classify Data for information based on the existing data available in the system; "Regression tree", which is used to make a forecast for predictions for future events based on the existing data in the system. Both of these trees are heavily used in machine learning algorithms. A widely used terminology for decision trees is "Classification and Regression trees" or "CART". Let's look at how you can build a simple decision tree based on a real-life example.

Step 1: Identify what decision needs to be made, which will serve as a "root node" for the decision tree. For this example, the decision needs to be made on "What would you like to do over the weekend?". Unlike real trees, the decision tree has its roots on top instead of the bottom.

Step 2: Identify conditions or influencing factors for your decision, which will serve as "branch nodes" for the decision tree. For this example, conditions could include "would you like to spend the weekend alone or with your friends?" and "how is the weather going to be?".

Step 3: As you answer the conditional questions, you may run into additional conditions that you might have ignored. You will now continue to your final decision by processing all the conditional questions individually; these bifurcations will serve as "edges" of your decision tree.

Step 4: Once you have processed all of the permutations and combinations and eventually made your final decision, that final decision will serve as the "leaf node" of your decision tree. Unlike "branch nodes", there are no further bifurcations possible from a "leaf node".

Here is the graphical representation of your decision for the example above:

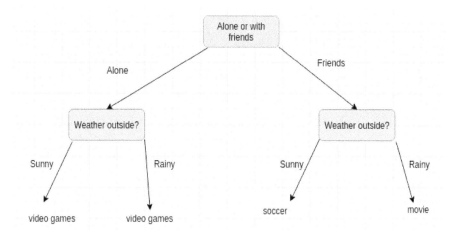

As you would expect from a decision tree, you have obtained a "model representing a set of sequential and hierarchical decisions that ultimately lead to some final decision". This example is at a very high-level to help you develop an understanding of the concept of decision trees. The data science and machine learning decision trees are much more complicated and bigger with hundreds and thousands of branch nodes and edges. The best tool on the market to visualize and understand decision trees is "Scikit Learn". Machine learning decisions tree models can be developed using two steps: "Induction" and "Pruning".

Induction

In this step, the decision trees are actually developed by selecting and modeling all of the sequential and hierarchical decision boundaries on the basis of the existing data set. For your ease of understanding, here are 4 high level steps required to develop the tree:

1. Gather, classify, and label the training data set with "feature variables" and "classification or regression output".

2. Identify the best and most cost effective feature within the training data set that will be used as the point for bifurcating the data.

3. Based on the possible values of the selected "best feature", create sub sets of data by bifurcating the data set. These bifurcations will define the "branch nodes" of the decision tree, wherein each node serves as a point of bifurcation based on specific features from the data set.

4. Iteratively develop new tree nodes with the use of data subsets gathered from step 3. These bifurcations will continue until an optimal point is reached, where maximum accuracy is achieved while minimizing the number of bifurcations or nodes.

Pruning

The inherent purpose of decision trees is to support training and self learning of the system, which often requires overloading of all possible conditions and influencing factors that might affect the final result. To overcome the challenge of setting the correct output for the least number of instances per node, developers make a "safe bet" by settling for that "least number" as rather small. This results in a high number of bifurcations on necessary, making for a very complex and large decision tree. This is where "tree pruning" comes into the picture. The verb "prune" literally means "to reduce especially by eliminating superfluous matter". This is the same kind of concept taken from real life tree pruning and applied to the data science and machine learning decision tree pruning process. The process of pruning effectively reduces the overall complexity of the decision tree by "transforming and compressing strict and rigid decision boundaries into generalized and smooth boundaries". The number of bifurcations in the decision trees determines the overall complexity of the tree. The easiest and widely used pruning method is reviewing individual branch nodes and evaluating the effect of its removal on the cost function of the decision tree. If the cost function has little to no effect of the removal, then the branch node under review can be easily removed or "pruned".

Advantages of Decision Trees

- Decision trees offer high transparency and can be easily understood and interpreted.
- Easily assess the influence of values of the features on the generated output.

- Gather a complete understanding of data accuracies and sources of error.

- Unlike most of the machine learning models, decision trees require the least amount of pre-processing of the data and can be used right out of the box with few adjustments made to the selective parameters.

- The number of data points used to train the tree is inversely proportional to the cost of gathering inferences from the tree.

Disadvantages of decision trees

- Considering the inherent nature of the training trees, overloading can easily occur.

- Decision trees can potentially become biased to the features with a majority of data points in the data set.

- Decision trees can be unreliable. Even a small wrong variation made to the data can result in the development of a completely different tree than needed. This is also called as "variance" and can be managed using methods like "bagging" and "boosting".

- "Greedy algorithms" cannot guarantee the return of the "globally optimal" decision tree. To mitigate this issue, multiple trees should be created and trained by randomly selecting the data features and samples from the training data set.

Random Forest

This is another type of supervised learning algorithm utilizing the ensemble learning technique for regressions and classification. Multiple decision trees will run simultaneously in a random forest with no interactions. Therefore, the bagging technique is employed on the dataset. This algorithm will construct a number of decision trees during the training phase and output the class that can either be the mean of all the predictions generated by each tree (regression) or mode of the classes created (classification). In 1995, Tin Kam Ho used the random subspace technique to develop the 1st random forest algorithm in an attempt to implement the stochastic discrimination approach. This algorithm was further enhanced by Adele Cutler and Leo Breiman, who ended up registering "Random Forests" as a trademark. This enhancement combined the bagging technique proposed by Breiman with randomly selecting predictive features as proposed by Ho. According to Ho, the random forest that splits with oblique hyperplanes are capable of gaining accuracy through the development without any need of additional training if the algorithm is randomly restricted to be responsive only to select feature dimensions. With the random subspace selection technique, a random forest of trees is grown and any variation among the trees will be introduced with training data projections into a random subspace. After this, every decision tree or node of the forest will undergo fitting. Since the random forest is capable of combining results of a number of predictions, it is considered a meta-estimator that can aggregate multiple decision trees. With certain required modifications listed below the trees can be prevented from high correlation.

1. Hyperparameter can be defined, which dictates the number of features that can be divided at each node as a predefined percentage of the total features. This will ensure that the ensemble model will not be too dependent on a single predictive feature and account for all features with no preference.

2. Every single tree will draw a sample from the dataset randomly while creating the splits and

further incorporating the element of randomness that would prevent overfitting of the model.

Random forest predictors are inherently inclined to dissimilarity in the observations starting with their development phase. The initial raw data set which has not been organized and labeled forms the observed data; on the other hand, the synthetic data can be extracted from a reference distribution. A "random forest dissimilarity measure" can be defined for unlabeled data allowing construction of a random forest predictor that can differentiate the observed data from a reference distribution. This dissimilarity measure equips the forest to process mixed variable types with high efficiency while accounting for the observation outliers and low variant inputs. It can also deal with a large volume of semi continuous variable owing to its internal variable selection. For instance, the image below contains 9 decision tree classifiers that will yield a random forest model combining inputs from all the 9 classifiers.

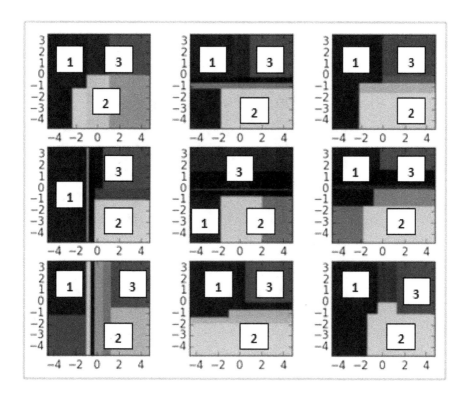

Now imagine, that the horizontal axis of these outputs are features P1 and the vertical axis as P2. The output was classified as select colors such as "blue" (1), "green" (2), "red" (3), and more. These outputs can then be combined by averaging the model votes into one ensemble model that will report higher performance than any single tree. The combined result of all the 9 trees is shown in the picture below:

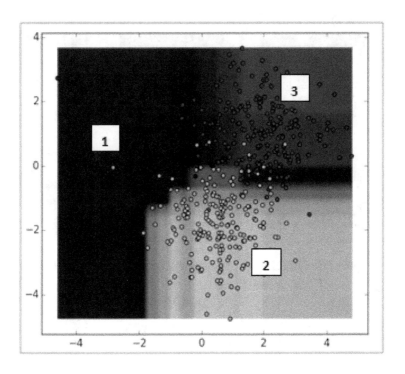

Advantages of Random Forest

- The accuracy of the resulting model is much higher than most of the other algorithms. It is also capable of producing dataset classifier with high accuracy.

- It can be executed on a big database with high efficiency.

- It is capable of handling a large volume of input variables with no deleted variables.

- It is capable of estimating variables that are significant in the classification.

- It will be able to generate an internal estimation of the generalization error with no bias as the model is being constructed.

- It is a highly effective technique to estimate missing data values and maintain reasonable accuracy even when a major portion of the data is missing.

Disadvantages of Random Forest

- The random forest algorithm can reportedly cause overfitting for certain dataset that constitutes of regression or classification tasks with significant background noise.

- When working with data containing categorical variables with multiple levels, random forests will be biased in favor of attributes with higher number of levels. As a result, the variable importance score that will be generated are unreliable for such a dataset.

Now, let's look at the steps required to implement random forest regression on a real life dataset.

1.   First, you need to import the required Python libraries and the dataset into a data frame using the code below.

"import pandas as pd
import numpy as np
import matplotlib.pyplot as plt"

"df = pd.read_csv ('Position_Salary.csv')"

2.   In this step, the dataset will be divided into training and test subsets in the Scikit-Learn library, using the code below.

"from   sklearn.model_selection   import train_test_split
X_train, X_test, Y_train, Y_test = train_test_split (X, Y, test_size = 0.2, random_state = 0)"

3.   Now, you can create a random forest regression model and fit it into the training data subset. You can select the desired number of trees by declaring the estimator. For this model, we will be using 11 trees by declaring n_estimator = 11, using the code below.

"from sklearn.ensemble import RandomForestRegressor

regressor = RandomForestRegressor (n_estimators = 11, random_state = 0)

regressor.fit (X.reshape (-1, 1), y.reshape (-1, 1))"

4.   This final step will produce the regression output, as shown in the picture below.

"X_grid = np.arrange (min (X), max (X), 0.01)

X_grid = X_grid.reshape ((len (X_grid), 1))

plt.scatter (X, Y, color = 'red')

plt.plot (X_grid, regressor.predict (X_grid), color = 'blue')

plt.title ('Truth or Bluff (Random Forest Regression)')

plt.xlabel ('Position level')

plt.ylabel ('Salary')

plt.show ( )"

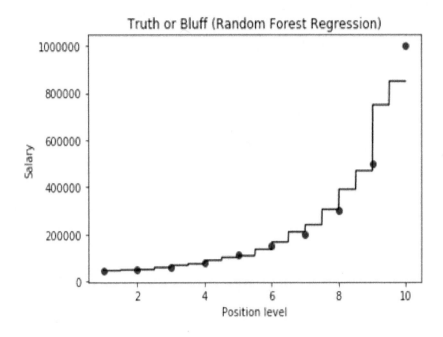

Day 6: Data Analysis Libraries

Data Analysis libraries are sensitive routines and functions that are written in any given language. Software developers require a robust set of libraries to perform complex tasks without needing to rewrite multiple lines of code. Machine learning is largely based on mathematical optimization, probability, and statistics.

Python is the language of choice in the field of data analysis and machine learning credited to consistent development time and flexibility. It is well suited to develop sophisticated models and production engines that can be directly plugged into production systems. One of its greatest assets being an extensive set of libraries that can help researchers who are less equipped with developer knowledge to easily execute data analysis and machine learning.

Scikit-Learn

"Scikit-Learn" has evolved as the gold standard for machine learning using Python, offering a wide variety of "supervised and unsupervised machine learning algorithms". It is touted as one of the most user-friendly and cleanest machine learning libraries to date. For example, decision trees, clustering, linear and logistics regressions and K-means. Scikit-learn uses a couple of basic Python libraries: NumPy and SciPy and adds a set of algorithms for data mining tasks including classification, regression, and clustering. It is also capable of implementing tasks like feature selection, transforming data and ensemble methods in only a few lines.

In 2007, David Cournapeau developed the foundational code of "Scikit-Learn" as part of a "Summer of Code" project for "Google". Scikit-learn has become one of Python's most famous open-source machine learning libraries since its launch in 2007. But it wasn't until 2010 that Scikit-Learn was released for public use. Scikit-Learn is "an open-sourced and BSD licensed, data mining and data analysis tool used to develop supervised and unsupervised machine learning algorithms" build on Python". Scikit-learn offers various "machine learning algorithms" such as "classification", "regression", "dimensionality reduction", and "clustering". It also offers modules for feature extraction, data processing, and model evaluation.

Prerequisites for application of Scikit-Learn library

The "Scikit-Learn" library is based on the "SciPy (Scientific Python)", which needs to be installed before using "SciKit-Learn.

SciPy (Fundamental library for scientific computing)

SciPy is a "collection of mathematical algorithms and convenience functions built on the NumPy extension of Python", capable of adding more impact to interactive Python sessions by offering high-level data manipulation and visualization commands and courses for the user. An interactive Python session with SciPy becomes an environment that rivals data processing and system prototyping technologies, including "MATLAB, IDL, Octave, R-Lab, and SciLab".

Another advantage of developing "SciPy" on Python, is the accessibility of a strong programming language in the development of advanced programs and specific apps. Scientific apps using SciPy benefit from developers around the globe, developing extra modules in countless software landscape niches. Everything produced has been made accessible to the Python programmer, from database subroutines and classes as well as "parallel programming to the web". These powerful tools are provided along with the "SciPy" mathematical libraries.

SymPy (Symbolic mathematics)

Developed by Ondřej Čertík and Aaron Meurer, SymPy is "an open-source Python library for symbolic computation". It offers algebra computing abilities to other apps, as a stand-alone app and/or as a library as well as live on the internet applications with "SymPy Live" or "SymPy Gamma". "SymPy" is easy to install and test, owing to the fact that it is completely developed in Python boasting limited dependencies.

SymPy involves characteristics ranging from calculus, algebra, discrete mathematics, and quantum physics to fundamental symbolic arithmetic. The outcome of the computations can be formatted as the "LaTeX" code. In combination with a straightforward, expandable codebase in a widespread programming language, the ease of access provided by SymPy makes it a computer algebra system with a comparatively low entry barrier.

NumPy (Base n-dimensional array package)

"NumPy" is the basic package with Python to perform scientific computations. It includes, among other things: "a powerful N-dimensional array object; sophisticated (broadcasting) functions; tools for integrating C/C++ and Fortran code; useful linear algebra, Fourier transform, and random number capabilities". The predecessor of NumPy called "Numeric" was initially developed by Jim Hugunin. In 2005, Travis Oliphant developed "NumPy" by integrating the functionalities of the "Numarray" into "Numeric" and making additional enhancements to it. NumPy is widely reckoned as an effective multi-dimensional container of generic data in addition to its apparent scientific uses. It is possible to define arbitrary data types. This enables NumPy to integrate with a wide variety of databases seamlessly and quickly. NumPy assists the "CPython reference implementation" of Python, which is a "non-optimizing bytecode interpreter". NumPy can partially address the issue of slow execution of mathematical algorithms, by offering multidimensional arrays, functions, and operators that work effectively on arrays by rewriting the code pertaining to the internal loops using NumPy.

Python bindings of "OpenCV's" commonly used computer vision library uses "NumPy arrays" for data storage and operation. Since pictures with various channels are merely depicted as 3-D arrays, indexing, slicing, or masking with other arrays are highly effective methods to access relevant pixels of the picture. The "NumPy array" as a universal data structure in "OpenCV" for pictures, extracted functionality points, filter kernels and several other to simplify the "programming workflow and debugging". The primary objective of NumPy is the homogeneity of the multidimensional array. It consists of an element table (generally numbers), all of which are of the same sort and are indicated by tuples of non-negative integers.

The dimensions of NumPy are called "axes", and the array class is called "ndarray". These arrays are considered "stridden views on memory". Unlike the built-in list data structure of Python (also a dynamic array), the "NumPy arrays" can be typed uniformly which means that "all the elements of a single array must be of the same type". Such arrays could also be "views of memory buffers assigned to the CPython interpreter by C / C++, Cython, and Fortran extensions without the need to copy data around", making them compatible with current numerical libraries. The "SciPy package" that incorporates a multitude of such libraries (particularly "BLAS" and "LAPACK") utilizes this capability. NumPy also offers built-in support for "memory-mapped ndarrays".

To develop "NumPy array" from "Python lists" while accessing elements, use the code below:

```
"import numpy as np

a = np.array([1, 2, 3])
print(type(a))
print(a.shape)
print(a[0], a[1], a[2])
a[0] = 5
print(a)

b = np.array([[1,2,3],[4,5,6]])
print(b.shape)
print(b[0, 0], b[0, 1], b[1, 0])"
```

Now, if you would like to index the "NumPy arrays", you should start with slicing the multidimensional "array" into one dimension with the code below:

```
"import numpy as np

a = np.array([[1,2,3,4], [5,6,7,8], [9,10,11,12]])
b = a[:2, 1:3]
print(a[0, 1])
b[0, 0] = 77
print(a[0, 1]) "
```

This will result in a "sub-array" of the original "NumPy array" but if you would like to generate an "arbitrary array", you can do so by utilizing "integer array indexing" which enables the generation of arbitrary arrays with the data from another array, as shown in the code below:

```
"import numpy as np

a = np.array([[1,2], [3, 4], [5, 6]])
print(a[[0, 1, 2], [0, 1, 0]])
print(np.array([a[0, 0], a[1, 1], a[2, 0]]))
print(a[[0, 0], [1, 1]])
```

print(np.array([a[0, 1], a[0, 1]]))"

Basic mathematical operations can be applied to arrays, as shown in the code below and can be found in "NumPy" as "functions" and "operator overloads".

```
"import numpy as np

x = np.array([[1,2],[3,4]], dtype=np.float64)
y = np.array([[5,6],[7,8]], dtype=np.float64)

print(x + y)
print(np.add(x, y))

print(x - y)
print(np.subtract(x, y))

print(x * y)
print(np.multiply(x, y))

print(x / y)
print(np.divide(x, y))

print(np.sqrt(x))"
```

Matplotlib (Comprehensive 2D/3D plotting)

"Matplotlib" is a 2-dimensional graphic generation library from Python that produces high-quality numbers across a range of hardcopy formats and interactive environments. The "Python script", the "Python", "IPython shells", the "Jupyter notebook", the web app servers, and select user interface toolkits can be used with matplotlib. Matplotlib attempts to further simplify easy tasks and make difficult tasks feasible. With only a few lines of code, you can produce tracks, histograms, scatter plots, bar graphs, error graphs, etc.

A MATLAB-like interface is provided for easy plotting of the Pyplot Module, especially when coupled with IPython. As a power user, you can regulate the entire line styles, fonts properties, and axis properties through an object-oriented interface or a collection of features similar to the one provided to MATLAB users.

Seaborn (data visualization)

Seaborn is derived from the Matplotlib Library and an extremely popular visualization library. It is a high-level library that can generate specific kinds of graph including heat maps, time series and violin plots.

Pandas (Data structures and analysis)

Pandas provide highly intuitive and user-friendly high-level data structures. "Pandas" has achieved popularity in the machine learning algorithm developer community, with built-in techniques for data aggregation, grouping, and filtering as well as results of time series analysis. The Pandas library has two primary structures: one-dimensional "Series" and two-dimensional "Data Frames".

Some of the key features provided by "Pandas" are listed below:

- A quick and effective "Data Frame object" with embedded indexing to be used in data manipulation activities.

- Tools to read and write data between internal memory data structures and multiple file formats, such as "CSV" and text, "Microsoft Excel", "SQL databases", and quick "HDF5 format".

- Intelligent data alignment and integrated management of incomplete data by achieving automatic label driven computational alignment and readily manipulating unorganized data into an orderly manner.

- Flexible reconstructing and pivoting of datasets.
- Smart label-based slicing and indexing of big data sets, as well as the creation of data subsets.
- Columns can be added to and removed from data structures to achieve the desired size of the database.
- Aggregation or transformation of data using a sophisticated "Group By" system enabling the execution of the "split-apply-combine" technique on the data.
- Highly efficient merge and join functions of the data set.
- "Hierarchical axis indexing" offers a simple way to work in a low dimensional data structure even with high dimensional data.
- Time-series functionalities, including "date range generation and frequency conversion, moving window statistics, moving window linear regressions, date shifting, and lagging". Also the creation of "domain-specific time offsets" and capability of joining time series with no data loss.

- Having most of the underlying code in "Cython" or "C", Pandas boasts high performance and efficiency.
- Python, in combination with Pandas, is being used in a broad range of academic and industrial sectors including Financial Services, Statistics, Neurobiology, Economics, Marketing and Advertising, Online Data Analytics, among others.

The two types of Data Structures offered by Pandas are: "Pandas DataFrame" and "Pandas Series".

Pandas DataFrame

It is defined as a "2-D labeled data structure with columns of a potentially different type". It has a high resemblance to the Excel spreadsheet as shown in the picture below, with multiple similar features for analysis, modification, and extraction of valuable insights from the data. You can create a "Pandas DataFrame" by entering datasets from "Excel", "CSV", and "MySQL database" among others.

	NAME	AGE	DESIGNATION
1	a	20	VP
2	b	27	CEO
3	c	35	CFO
4	d	55	VP
5	e	18	VP
6	f	21	CEO
7	g	35	MD

For instance, in the picture above assume "Keys" are represented by the name of the columns and "Values" are represented by the list of items in that column, a "Python dictionary" can be used to represent this as shown in the code below:

```
"my_dict = {
    'name' : ["a", "b", "c", "d", "e"",f", "g"],
    'age' : [20,27, 35, 55, 18, 21, 35],
    'designation': ["VP", "CEO", "CFO", "VP", "VP",
"CEO", "MD"]
    }"
```

The "Pandas DataFrame" can be created from this dictionary by using the code below:

```
"import Pandas as PD
```

df = pd.DataFrame(my_dict)"

The resulting "DataFrame" is shown in the picture below which resembles the excel spreadsheet:

	age	designation	name
0	20	VP	a
1	27	CEO	b
2	35	CFO	c
3	55	VP	d
4	18	VP	e
5	21	CEO	f
6	35	MD	g

If you would like to define index values for the rows, you will have to add the "index" parameter in the "DataFrame ( )" clause as shown below:

"df = pd.DataFrame(my_dict, index=[1,2,3,4,5,6,7])"

To obtain "string" indexes for the data instead of numeric, use the code below:

"df = pd.DataFrame(

my_dict,

*index=["First", "Second", "Third", "Fourth", "Fifth",
"Sixth", "Seventh"]*

)"

Now, as these index values are uniform, you could execute the code below to utilize the "NumPy arrays" as index values:

"np_arr = np.array([10,20,30,40,50,60,70])
df = pd.DataFrame(my_dict, index=np_arr)"

Similar to "NumPy", the columns of "DataFrame" are also homogeneous. You can use dictionary like syntax or add the column name with "DataFrame", to view the data type of the column, as shown in the code below:

"df['age'].dtype   # Dict Like Syntax
df.age.dtype   # DataFrame.ColumnName
df.name.dtype   # DataFrame.ColumnName"

You can use the code below to selectively view the record or rows available within the "Pandas DataFrame", by using the "head ( )" function for the first five rows and "tail ( )" function for the last five rows. For instance, use the code below to view the first 3 rows of the data:

```
"df.head(3)   # Display first 3 Rows"
```

Pandas Series

It can be defined as a "one-dimensional labeled array capable of holding data of any type (integer, string, float, python objects)". Simply put, it is like a column in an excel spreadsheet. To generate a "Pandas Series" from an array, a "NumPy" module must be imported and used with "array ()" function, as shown in the code below:

```
"# import pandas as pd
import pandas as pd"

"# import numpy as np
import numpy as np"

"# simple array
data = np.array (['m','a','c','h','I','n','e'])"

"ser = pd.Series(data)
print(ser)"
```

IPython (Enhanced interactive console)

"IPython (Interactive Python)" is an interface or command shell for interactive computing using a variety of programming languages. "IPython" was initially created exclusively for Python, which supports introspection, rich media, shell syntax, tab completion, and history. Some of the functionalities provided by IPython include: "interactive shells (terminal and Qt-based); browser-based notebook interface with code, text, math, inline plots and other media support; support for interactive data visualization and use of GUI tool kits; flexible interpreters that can be embedded to load into your own projects; tools for parallel computing". The architecture of "IPython" offers "parallel and distributed computing". IPython" allows the development, execution, debugging and interactive monitoring of parallel applications, thus the "I (Interactive) in IPython". The underlying architecture can easily separate parallelism, allowing "IPython" to assist with multiple parallelism styles including: "Single program, various information (SPMD) parallelism", "Multiple programs, various data (MIMD) parallelism", "Message passing using MPI", "Task parallelism", "Data parallelism", combinations of these methods and even customized user-defined strategies.

The parallel computing functionality has been rendered optional under the "ipyparallel python package", with the implementation of "IPython 4.0".

"IPython" often derives from "SciPy stack libraries" such as "NumPy" and "SciPy", frequently installed in combination with one of the various "Scientific Python distributions". IPython" can also be integrated with select "SciPy stack libraries", primarily "matplotlib", which produces inline charts upon use with the "Jupyter notebook". For customization of rich object display, Python libraries can be implemented with "IPython-specific hooks". For instance, if used in the context of "IPython", "SymPy" can implement "rendering of mathematical expressions as rendered LaTeX".

Jupyter Notebook

The Jupyter Notebook (JN) is widely regarded as one of the most powerful applications that allow the development and presentation of data science projects in a highly interactive manner. The "notebook" in the name refers to its advance feature that allows integration of the code and outputs into one comprehensive document, combining visuals, narrated texts, math equations and other rich media. As a result of this intuitive workflow, you can perform sequential development in a short period of time. In 2010, the prototype of IPython Notebook was published and eventually succeeded by the Jupyter Notebook. To be able to use JN, you can simply install the "Anaconda" data science package, which contains some of the most powerful Python based libraries and tools including Matplotlib, Pandas and NumPy. You can download the latest version of this tool from the official "Anaconda Cloud" website and follow the step by step guide for installation instructions. If you already have Python installed on your operating system, you can execute the pip file below to operate JN:

"pip3 install jupyter"

Now, if you are operating the Windows system, then you will be able to access Jupyter by clicking on the shortcut button for "Anaconda" that would be added to the start menu. A new tab containing the Jupyter Notebook dashboard will open in your computer's default browser, as shown in the picture below. You will be able to create and manage all your JN from this dashboard and edit them as needed. The JN dashboard and all the notebooks are web based applications that will be accessible through your browser using a local Python server. This feature renders the JN independent of the platform itself and allows for easy online sharing.

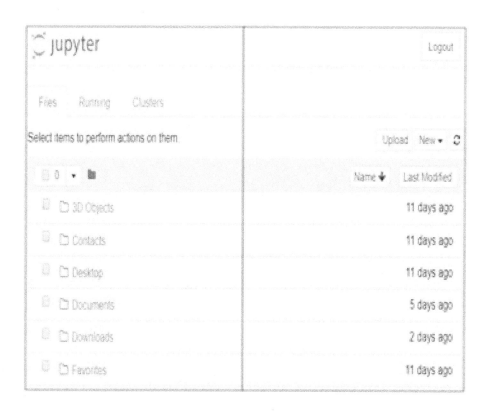

Click on the "New" icon and a drop down menu will be displayed. Simply select your Python version or "Python 3" and just like that, you have created your first Jupyter Notebook. The notebook would be displayed in a new tab and the dashboard will now have a new file labeled "untitled.ipynb". Every ".ipynb" text file will describe the contents of the notebook in "JSON" format. You will be able to view all the attached images, cells and underlying content that has been converted into text format along with the available metadata.

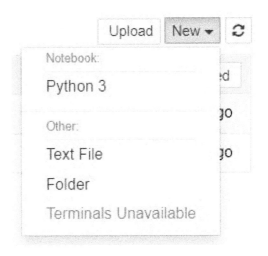

You will not be able to change the name of the notebook from the JN application directly. You can use either the file browser or leverage the dashboard to give the desired name to your notebook. The first step is to shut the running notebook by clicking on "File", then selecting "Close and Halt" from the menu bar. Alternatively, you can terminate the run by selecting the notebook from the dashboard and selecting "Shutdown". Remember you will not be able to terminate the run by simply closing the browser tab running the notebook. The kernel will continue to be executed in the background. Now that your notebook is no longer running select "Rename" from the dashboard and enter the desired name for your notebook. The JN interface containing your newly created notebook will look similar to the picture shown below. A lot of options on the interface are similar to a standard word processor. The two unique features are "Cell" and "Kernel". "Kernel" is the engine executing all the computations and code that have been written in the notebook. On the other hand, "Cell" refers to the code that will be executed in the kernel and serves as a container for the strings that will be displayed in the notebook.

Jupyter Notebook Cells

There are 2 types of cells that you must remember:

- **Code cell** – Holds the code that is ready for execution within a kernel and will then display the resulting output.

- **Markdown cell** – Hold any texts that have been edited using markdown feature and then displaying the resulting output upon execution.

The cell at the first position of any notebook is defaulted to be a code cell. Let's look at the code below for displaying the desired text by typing it into the first cell and clicking on the "Run" button on the toolbar.

print ('Happy New Year!')

Output – Happy New Year!

As the code is executed, the label on the left will be modified from "In [ ]" to "In [1]" and the output would be added to the notebook. The "In" of the label pertains to the input and the numeric value of the label denoted the position at which the cell went through execution on the kernel. This denotes the key difference between code cells (no label) and markdown cells (contain a label at its left). If the code is executed again, then the label will change to "In [2]".

The cells that are being executed will have a blue border surrounding them; on the other hand, the active cells that are being edited will have a green border around them. For the creation of any new code cells, you can click on "Insert" on the menu bar, then click on "Insert Cell Below" and write any code that you would like to execute. For example, if you execute the code below no output will be produced but the label of the cell will be changed to "In [*]" indicating that the cell is currently under execution (taking 4 seconds as specified).

import time

time.sleep (4)

Markdown is a markup language that lets you format plain text using a syntax similar to HTML (Hypertext Markup Language) tags. The sample code below in the Jupyter Notebook was written in Markup cells.

 # Title Text 1

Subtitle Text 2

You can type in desired plain text that will be displayed as a paragraph.

You can format the text to be displayed as italic or bold.

Every set of code divided by an empty line will form a separate paragraph.

You will be able to include lists.

*Indent the list using *.*

Use numbers to generate ordered lists.

1. This can be list 1.

2. This can be list 2.

You can also include hyperlinks by writing them as [hyperlink] (web url)

Inline codes will have single quote.

Block of codes will be written in triple quotes.

Images can be added, for example![Image text] (image web url)

Once this code has been executed, the paragraph above will be the resulting output. You can also add the image to the notebook using a local URL of the image or as an attachment by clicking on the "Edit" button and selecting "Insert Image" to convert the image into markup text which will be saved in the ".ipynb" file.

Jupyter Notebook Kernels

As mentioned earlier, the kernel allows the execution of the code and then returns the output to the cell for display. The state of the kernel remains the same between different cells and time periods since kernels are connected to the notebook as an entity and not the cells.

For instance, when libraries are imported or variables are declared in one cell, they can be accessed through other cells as well. A JN functions like a multimedia rich file. Let's look at the code below to understand further:

```
"import numpy as np
def square (x):
    return x * x"
```

The code above will import the NumPy package, and a function will be defined. Once this code has been executed, you can reference "np" and "square" functions through any cell in the notebook using the code below:

```
"x = np.random.randint (1, 10)
y = square (x)
print ('%d squared is %d' % (x, y))"
```

The code above would be executed independently of the order of the cells in the notebook. Conventionally the code in a Jupyter Notebook will be executed in a top-down flow but can be altered to execute any modifications. Cells will be executed starting from the left and any stale output would be indicated as well. Some of the menu options that can be used on Kernels are listed below:

1. **Restart** – This will let you restart the kernel so you will be able to clear all predefined variables and other input.

2. **Restart and Clear Output** – This will perform all the restart functions as well as the output shown below the code cells.

3. **Restart and Run All** – This will perform all the restart and clear output functions mentioned earlier. You will also be able to run all the cells starting with the first cell to the last one.

4. **Interrupt** – This will let you terminate the execution of any kernel if it encounters any errors.

A large number of kernels are available for various versions of Python and several programming languages such as C, Java, and many more. Every kernel will have its own set of installation guidelines that you can easily follow and run the required commands successfully.

Day 7: Predictive Analytics

According to SAS, customer analytics can be defined as "processes and technologies bad gives organizations the customer insight necessary to deliver offers that are anticipated, relevant and timely". Customer analytics is at the heart of all marketing activities and is an umbrella term used for techniques such as "predictive modeling", "data visualization", "information management", and "segmentation". The end to end the journey of a potential customer right from the point when they learn about or become aware of the company's product to eventually spending money to make a purchase is referred to as "marketing and the sales funnel". It is a visual representation of various routes taken and stages past by the customer to be converted into a product buyer. By carefully evaluating their marketing and sales funnel, companies can Drive up their sales increase their brand awareness and gain more loyal customers.

The concept of a marketing funnel has been derived from a classic "hierarchy of effects" model framework called "AIDA", which was introduced in the late 20th century by Elias St. Elmo Lewis. According to this business and customer relationship model, every new customer goes through four stages before making an actual purchase. The fundamentals of the marketing funnel have evolved from this model and largely remain the same. The beauty of the marketing funnel is that it can be easily customized for different companies across different industrial sectors to best meet their company vision and market demands. There isn't a single standard marketing funnel model that is universally accepted by all businesses. Companies choose and customize their own marketing model depending on the complexity and general awareness of their products and services. A relatively simple marketing funnel is referred to as "TOFU-MOFU-BOFU" model which stands for "top of the funnel, middle of the funnel and bottom of the funnel", representing the 3 Different stages of the marketing funnel adopted by the company.

With the rise in cutting edge technology, the everyday consumer has become smarter and expects more worth for their money. The loyalty of today's smart customer lies within the confines of the most engaging and enhanced user expedience supported by top notch Data privacy and security measures. People are not afraid to experiment with the new products and do away with the normal product choices that they might have used for years. This has resulted in a modification to the marketing funnel with marketing gurus proposing additional stages to the final namely, "Loyalty" and "Advocacy" to improve their overall marketing strategy. It is estimated that "businesses lose up to $1.6 trillion a year when their existing customers leave them".

Importance of Customer Analytics

Customer analytics has evolved as the backbone of the marketing industry. This is a direct result of the advent of "smart consumer" who is more aware and connected to one another than ever before and willing to take their business elsewhere at a moment's notice. The smart customer has seamless access to a variety of information including the best products and services available in the market and where can they find the best deals to make the most of their money. Therefore, companies are required it to be proactive and be able to predict consumer behavior when interacting with their products so as to be in a position to take the required action to convert the prospective customer into a paying client. To generate more accurate forecasts and predictions of customer behavior, companies must have a solid understanding of their customers buying habits and lifestyle choices. These near accurate predictions will provide the company with an edge over the competition and help achieve higher conversion rates in their sales and marketing funnel. One of the best customer analytics solution in the market today is "SAS Customer Intelligence", which claims to have the following applications:

- Achieve higher customer loyalty and response rates.

- Generate personalized customer offers and messages to reach the right customer at the right time.

- Identify prospective customers with similar attributes and high likelihood of conversion so the company can reduce costs on their targeted marketing strategies and campaigns.

- Reduce customer attrition by generating accurate predictions on customers that are more likely to take their business somewhere else and developing proactive marketing campaigns to retain them.

"The insights derived from our new analytics capabilities are allowing us to find the sweet spots that will continue to drive loyalty, profitability, and sustainable growth".

- Carrie Gray, Executive Director for Medium Business Marketing, Verizon

Marketing and Sales Funnel Analytics

Companies are always looking to grow and optimize their sales process taking into consideration all influencing factors such as the performance of their sales and marketing team, their sales pipeline and most importantly their sales and marketing funnel. The process of analyzing the conversion rate between different stages of the sales and marketing funnel is called as "sales funnel analytics". Companies primarily initiate their analysis at the top of the funnel and work their way down while calculating the conversion rates between subsequent stages. Some of the most widely used sales funnel analytics tool are:

"Google Analytics" – As you would expect, the "Google Analytics" platform is top-of-the-line with built in sales funnel analysis features. It allows companies to understand the interactions and engagement of the customers with their online content and mobile applications by visualizing robust dashboards and reports. The machine learning capabilities of this platform can be used to predict which customer is more likely to convert to a paying buyer and which customer has the potential to generate higher revenue.

"Google Analytics helped us optimize our art marketplace, resulting in 400% year-over-year revenue growth for our art business".
- Mariam Naficy, Founder & CEO, Minted

"Hotjar" – The "Hotjar" funnels are primarily used to generate heat maps for website traffics but also provide built in funnel metrics. It is highly customizable and capable of automatically refreshing the funnel data every hour.

"After looking at a lot of recordings, heat maps, and getting feedback from the polls, we got a good idea of what our users wanted and moved from around 80K members to now over 150k. Hotjar was a big piece of that redesign".
-   Inbound.org

"GetResponse Autofunnel" – Recently, the "GetResponse" company launched its new built in "Autofunnel" tool that can easily create a customized and automated sales funnel to meet specific business requirements. With this tool companies can automate their customer communication emails, develop website landing pages, recover abandoned orders and increase their customer conversion rate.

"With Autofunnel you can promote, sell, and deliver your products online with simple, effective sales funnels. Sell anything – a physical product, ebook, an online course – anything. Send traffic straight to your sales page with the quick sales funnel, or nurture new contacts with automated emails before presenting your offer with the full sales funnel".

- GetResponse

Predictive Analytics Marketing

According to SAS, predictive analytics is *"use of data, statistical algorithms and machine learning techniques to identify the likelihood of future outcomes based on historical data. The goal is to go beyond knowing what has happened to providing a best assessment of what will happen in the future"*. Today companies are digging through their past with an eye on the future, and this is where artificial intelligence for marketing comes into play, with the application of predictive analytics technology. The success of predictive analytics is directly proportional to the quality of big data collected by the company. Here are some of the widely used predictive analytics applications for marketing:

Predictive analysis for customer behavior

For the industrial giants like "Amazon", "Apple", and "Netflix", analyzing customer activities and behavior is fundamental to their day to day operations. Smaller businesses are increasingly following in their footsteps to implement predictive analysis in their business model. The development of a customized suite of predictive models for a company is not only capital-intensive but also requires extensive manpower and time. Marketing companies like "AgilOne" offer relatively simple predictive model types with wide applicability across industrial domains. They have identified three main types of predictive models to analyze customer behavior, which are:

"Propensity models" – These models are used to generate "true or accurate" predictions for customer behavior. Some of the most common propensity models include: "predictive lifetime value", "propensity to buy", "propensity to turn", "propensity to convert", "likelihood of engagement", and "propensity to unsubscribe".

"Cluster models" – These models are used to separate and group customers based on shared attributes such as gender, age, purchase history, and demographics. Some of the most common cluster models include: "product based or category based clustering", "behavioral customs clustering", and "brand based clustering".

"Collaborative filtering" – These models are used to generate products and services and recommendations as well as to recommended advertisements based on prior customer activities and behaviors. Some of the most common collaborative filtering models include: "up sell", "cross sell", and "next sell" recommendations. The most significant tool used by companies to execute predictive analytics on customer behavior is "regression analysis", which allows the company to establish correlations between the sale of a particular product and the specific attributes displayed by the purchasing customer. This is achieved by employing "regression coefficients", which are numeric values depicting the degree to which the customer behavior is affected by different variables, and developing a "likelihood score" for the future sale of the product.

Qualification and Prioritization of Leads

There are three primary categories employed in business to business or B2B predictive analytics marketing to qualify and prioritize prospective customers or "leads". These categories are:

"**Predictive scoring**" which is used to prioritize prospective customers on the basis of their likelihood to make an actual purchase

"**Identification models**" which are used to identify and acquire new prospective customers on the basis of attributes that are shared with the existing customers of the company.

"**Automated segmentation**", which is used to separate and classify prospective customers on the basis of shared attributes to be targeted with the same personalized marketing strategies and campaigns. The predictive analytics technology needs a large volume of sales data that serves as a building block and training material to increase the accuracy and efficiency of the predictive models. Small brick-and-mortar companies cannot afford to expand their computing resources. Therefore, are unable to efficiently collect customer behavioral data from their in-store sales. This translates into a competitive edge for larger companies with a more advanced computing system which exacerbates the superfluous growth of larger companies in comparison to small businesses.

Identification of current market trend

Companies can employ "data visualization" tools that allow business executives and managers to gather insights on the current state of the company, simply by visualizing their existing customer behavioral data on a "report or dashboard". These dashboard reports tend to inspire and generate customer behavior driven actions. For example, with the use of data visualization tools, a company can identify the underlying trend of customer demands in specific neighborhoods and accordingly plan to stock their inventory for individual stores. The same information can bring to light the best products and services for the company to be launched on the basis of the current market trends that can suffice the customer demands. The market trend insights can also be applied to increase the efficiency of a company's supply chain management model.

Customer segmentation and targeting

One of the simplest and highly effective ways of optimizing a product offer to achieve a rapid turnaround on the company's return on investment is the ability to target "right customers" with appropriate product offers at the "right time". This also happens to be the most common and widely used application of predictive analytics in the world of marketing. According to a research study conducted by the "Aberdeen Group", companies using predictive analytics in their marketing strategies are two times more likely to successfully identify "high value customers".

This is where the quality of the company's existing data set takes precedence. The highly recommended practice is to use historical consumer behavioral data of all existing customers and analyze it to segment and target customers with similar purchasing attributes with personalized recommendations and marketing campaigns.

Some of the most common predictive analytics models used and this application are "affinity analysis", "churn analysis", and "response modeling". Using these applications, companies can gather insight such as "if combining digital and print subscriptions of their product offerings or catalog is a good idea" or "whether their product or service will be more successful if offered as a monthly subscription model or one time purchase fee". One of the leading sales and marketing platform companies is "Salesforce", which offers a cloud based platform that can be used by businesses to generate customer profiles as a product of the data collected from independent sources, including customer relationship management (CRM) applications and other company applications. By selectively and mindfully adding inputted data to this platform, companies can seamlessly track their customer behavior to develop a customer behavioral model overtime that can feed into the company's decision-making process in real time and over the long term.

Development of marketing strategies

Another application of predictive analytics and marketing is providing access to a variety of customer related data such as data collected from social media platforms and the company's own internal structured data. The customer behavioral model can then be generated by collating all available data and applying "behavioral scoring" on it.

All the companies across different industrial sectors are required to adapt to changing or evolving customer behavior through proliferating marketing mediums or channels. For example, companies can use any of the predictive analytics model described above, to precisely predict if their planned marketing campaign would have more success on the social media platforms or on their mobile applications. Companies are able to employ a predictive analytics model to gain an understanding of how their customers are interacting with their products or services, based on their feelings or emotions shared on the social media platforms concerning a particular topic. This process is referred to as "sentiment analysis" or "text analysis".

Exploratory analysis of customer data

"Exploratory Data Analysis" or EDA provides a comprehensive view of existing customer data generated pertinent customer data sources such as product prices, current and historical customer surveys, product usage, purchase history, and demographics. It is considered as an approach to look at the data without the use of any statistical model and the data inferences. The term "Exploratory Data Analysis" was coined by John Tukey, in his book released in 1977. Some of the main reasons to use exploratory data analysis are:

- Preliminary selection of the applicable "predictive models".

- Verification of underlying assumptions.

- Make sure the company is asking the right questions to expand their customer base.

- Detect potential data anomalies, redundancies and errors.

- Determination of the relationship between the "explanatory variables".

- Assessment of the direction and size of the relationship between "explanatory variables" and "outcome variables".

The customer data collected in the database form of a rectangular array with individual columns for "subject identifier", "outcome variable", and "explanatory variable". It is rather challenging to look at a spreadsheet filled with numerical values and determine important information from the data and this is where exploratory data analysis techniques are used to selectively display important character is to of the data. There are four types of exploratory data analysis techniques:

1. **"Univariate non-graphical"** - This technique looks at a single variable or data column at a time and displays the results as a statistical summary.

2. **"Multivariate non- graphical"** - This technique looks at two or more variables or data columns at a time and displays the results as a statistical summary.

3. **"Univariate graphical"** - This technique looks at a single variable or data column at a time and displays the results diagrammatically or using pictorial graphs.

4. **"Multivariate graphical"** - This technique looks at two or more variables or data columns at a

time and displays the results diagrammatically or using pictorial graphs.

EDA helps in the determination of the best predictive model to address the business problem by generating a low risk and low cost comprehensive report of the data findings and solution recommendations for best suited customer data models. The in-depth exploratory analysis of customer behavior provides exposure to hidden data patterns and market trends that would have been easily lost in the mass of information. Some of the conclusions that can be derived using EDA on customer behavioral data are:

- Identification of customers with the highest number of purchases and the maximum amount of money spent.
- Finding the number of orders generated on a daily, weekly, and monthly basis.
- Identification of the distribution of the unit price for all company products.
- Identify purchase transaction patterns based on demographics and location of the customers.

Personalized marketing

In a research study sponsored by "Researchscape International", about 75% of the marketing agencies stated that personalize marketing has immensely held their companies and clients in advancing customer relationships and a whopping 97% stated that they will continue to invest in personalized marketing efforts. This is primarily driven by the fact that companies are able to effectively communicate with their target markets by gathering valuable insights from customer behavioral data using predictive analytics and machine learning algorithms. Typically, personalization starts from an individual customer but can potentially be applied to a segment of customers with shared attributes and achieve "personalization at scale".

Artificial intelligence based tools and applications can perform image recognition and voice analysis in combination with customer behavior analysis to provide companies a deeper understanding of customer demands and needs that can be met by delivering precise product recommendations. Here are some industrial applications of personalized marketing:

Ad targeting

Companies can target advertisements to a specific user or a segment of customers based on their shopping attributes such as recent views of a particular product or category and purchase history. Some of the Ad targeting applications available in the market are:

"ReFUEL4" – The "Ad Analyzer", developed by the marketing company "ReFUEL4", utilizes computer's visual capabilities to predict the performance of the advertisement. If the company's existing ad starts declining in performance, the ad analyzer can help the company to develop a new and better ad. The decline in ad performance typically signals audience fatigue, when people stop paying attention to the ad because it has become too familiar and uninteresting.

"Match2one" – This advertising application can be integrated into the company's e-commerce site and used to I've tracked prospective customers and retain existing customers. The "Match2One" application uses machine learning algorithms to target potential customers that have a higher likelihood of paying consumers. The company claims that it's "engine is trained to generate leads and find new customers using a combination of site visitor behavior and historical data". By analyzing the website visitor data, the application can show targeted ads to the customers hold displayed interest and in particular product.

Personalized messaging

The most important aspect of personalized messaging is contextual marketing. To make sure relevant messages are being sent to the target audience, companies gather customer data, including their behavior, webpage view history, preferred content, social media posts and demographics among other variables. Some of the personalized messaging application available in the market are:

"Dynamic yield" – The email solution provided by the company uses customer behavioral data such as order history, email clicks, social media activity, among other features to generate personalized email content for the individual customers. The email solution supplies dynamic email templates that can be easily customized to reflect relevant messages. This application is used across several industrial domains including travel, E-commerce, the gaming industry and social media.

"Yoochoose" – This company offers e-commerce services to online retailers that allow the company to create a "personalized shopping experience" for their consumers, using personalized emails or targeted notifications with newsletters and product recommendations that automatically triggered by customer behavior. The application is capable of identifying customers who have not made a purchase for some time and trigger a notification to remind them to make a purchase. It can also identify customers who have recently made a purchase and trigger an "after sale, thank you" email. The company offers the "target notifications" functionality along with a product recommendation engine and a "personalized search", all of which are packaged into a "personalization suite".

Product recommendations

The easiest and smartest read for any company to grow their business is to provide accurate product recommendations that are relevant to the needs and demands of the customer. Companies can also reduce the volume and frequency of product returns while increasing their income through new products, repeat purchases and retargeting to entice new potential customers and higher customer loyalty. Some of the product recommendations applications available in the market are:

"Recombee" – This application is based on advanced machine learning algorithms that are capable of generating recommendations within "200 milliseconds of the customer activity". The company claims that its application can generate over 500 recommendations per second, by employing a combination of "collaborative filtering algorithms" developed for customer behavioral analysis and "content based algorithms" to analyze product titles and descriptions. With every human interaction, the learning algorithms improves upon itself and continues to refine the recommendations with iterative use by the customer. This application is widely used in the real estate industry, job boards, classified ad, gaming industry, the travel industry and entertainment industry, among others.

"Sentient Aware" – The product recommendation engine offered by "Sentient Aware" analyzes consumer's Visual activity and behavioral interactions to activate the "deep learning algorithms" within the company website. This application utilizes "intent and curation driven algorithms" to identify similar products and the company catalog to generate predictions on customers Preferences and make product recommendations that align with those preferences. The company claims that it's application is just as efficient at recommending products for first-time users owing to its capability to generate recommendations without using historical data.

Dynamic websites

A website that can cater to individual site preferences of every customer on-the-fly by dynamically changing its content, which is driven by underlying scripts, is called a "dynamic website". The repetitive tasks including tagging photos and rendering photos, are carried out using artificial intelligence technologies such as "image recognition" and "machine learning". Some of the dynamic website applications available in the market today are:

"Bookmark" – The company "Bookmark" has successfully applied Machine learning technology to web design. The company claims that its "AI Design Assistant" or (AIDA) can custom build company websites pertaining to various website elements, sections, and images as well as the overall web design that should feature on the site based on the company's industry specific information. "AIDA" is capable of searching the Internet to gather more information about the client company by running a search on the company name location and type of business. This application collects information on the client's customer behavior and activity on social media and analyzes that information to determine the best website elements and design for the company's e-commerce platform.

"LiftIgniter" –The dynamic website recommendation system developed by "LiftIgniter", can be directly integrated with the client's e-commerce platforms online and on mobile applications and is driven by the machine learning algorithm called "true parallel multivariate algorithms infrastructure". This integrated system learns from the customer interactions with the e-commerce platforms and sifts through all of the company's online content to display recommended products within 150 milliseconds, that the customer might be interested in, based on their real time activity on the platform.

Extra content

Python Data Science: An hands-on introduction to big data analysis and data mining, a project-based guide with practical exercises (Book 3) has been structured as a 7-day-course with seven chapter (one per day), to guide the reader in a journey into the huge worl of Python.

The journey is thought and structured by Computer Programming Academy as a month long course. So it is just began!

This book is part of a series with other two:

- *Python Programming: An hands-on introduction to computer programming and algorithms, a project-based guide with practical exercises (Book 1)*
- *Python Machine Learning: An hands-on introduction to artificial intelligence coding, a project-based guide with practical exercises (Book 2)*

Here below a free sneak peak of Book 1 *Python Programming* and Book 2 *Python Machine Learning*, enjoy!

Python programming: An hands-on introduction to computer programming and algorithms, a project-based guide with practical exercises (Book 1)

This book will discuss various fundamental concepts of the Python programming language. There are 7 chapters in this book, crafted specifically to help you master basic and advanced python programming concepts required to develop web based programs and applications in just a week.

The first chapter of this book starts with an introduction to computer programming and some of the most widely used programming languages. You will also learn the fundamental elements of computer programming language such as basic operators, functions, decision making, among others. The importance of mathematical concepts such as algebra and statistics in computer programming has also been explained. Chapter 2 will provide a detailed overview of Python and its historical development. Step by step instructions to install Python on your operating systems have also been included. The concept of Python comments, variables and data types that serve as a prerequisite to the learning of Python programming have been explained in detail.

Chapter 3 is a detailed overview of the basic concepts of Python programming focusing on various programming elements such as Booleans, Tuples, Sets, Dictionaries and much more. The nuances of how to write efficient and effective Python codes have been explained in detail along with plenty of examples and sample exercises to help you solidify your understanding of these concepts. Chapter 4 pertains to the advance Python programming concepts that are relatively more complicated and require a solid understanding of the basic concepts. You will learn how to use OOPS concepts, different loops and conditional statements to generate sophisticated commands. This chapter also includes plenty of examples and sample exercises so you can verify what you have learned.

Like most programming languages, Python boasts a number of built-in functions to make your life easier while coding a software program. Chapter 5 contains a list of all such built-in functions, methods and keywords that can be used to easily develop and run advance codes. Chapter 6 will provide a detailed overview of Django which is web framework that is popularly used in the development of web based programs and applications. You will learn how to install Django on your computer and follow the step by step coding instructions to develop your own web based program and notes taking application.

The final chapter, "Python Applications", will provide details on how Python programming is being used in the development and testing of software programs, machine learning algorithms and Artificial Intelligence technologies to solve real world problems. These cutting edge technologies have resulted in tools and programs that are being utilized across the industrial spectrum to solve real world problems and become more futuristic. This chapter also includes various Python programming tips and tricks that will help you take your coding skills to the next level.

Day 1: Computer Programming 101

Humans have evolved their medium of communication over centuries, resulting in a wide variety of languages spoken across the world. However, all manmade languages have a shared set of features that are remarkably standard across the board. Every language has a script containing different parts of a structured sentence such as nouns, verbs, adjectives, and other elements.

This is where we can draw a bridge to the computer programming languages, which are also composed of a variety of fundamental elements. We will look at each of these elements in detail later in this chapter. However, computer languages allow humans to interact with and guide the computing machines to perform desired operations. It allows the development and implementation of advance computing technologies. These programming languages also allow computers to interact with one another.

Here is a quick overview of some of the most popular computer programming languages.

C

C Language can be defined as a structure-oriented (functions are stored as a self-contained unit), medium level programming language widely utilized in the development of "low-level" applications (pertaining to hardware components of the computer). In 1972, Bell Laboratories developed the C language for implementation in the UNIX system. A number of sophisticated and advanced programming languages such as Java, JavaScript, C++, C# and Perl are derived from the "grandmother" C language. Until the introduction of Java, the C language was the most dominant high-level language of the industry. Some of the only operating systems like IBM System/370 were also developed using the C language. The C language is rated low on the scale of learning difficulty primarily owing to the limited number of keywords,32, that need to be trained on, and thus, it often serves as a foundational language for coding beginners. It is often used for the development of software applications that require integration to an operating system like UNIX, Linux and Windows. Some of the most popular C language based applications are: Word processors, OS development, database systems, network drivers and interpreters, compilers and assemblers, spreadsheets and graphics packages. Facebook's TAO systems are developed using the C language.

C++

Developed in 1983 as an extension of the C language, C++ can be defined as an object oriented (grouping of function and the associated dataset into an object), "medium level" (interacting with the programming layer of the computer) programming language that can be used for the development of general purpose software. It allows coding in similar syntax as the C language making C++ a perfect example of a "hybrid language". The C++ language with a robust standard library and (STL) quick processing and compilation mechanism, is used to develop various application suites such as "Microsoft Office", graphics editing tools, video editors, gaming packages and even entire Operating Systems. The "BlackBerry" operating system and the latest Microsoft Office suite are developed entirely on the C++ language.

The C++ language is widely perceived as the enhanced version of the C language with object oriented up to approach that can be used to generate efficient and lean code. It also provides a high level of abstraction to allow improved management of large development projects. The C++ language tends to be the first programming language taught at college level. Some of the major companies and organizations using C++ are Amazon, Google, Adobe software, Mozilla, Winamp, and Lockheed Martin. The C++ language is specifically used in the development of Embedded Firmware, Client Server Applications, Drivers, and system programs.

C#

In 2000, Microsoft released C# (pronounced as C-sharp) as part of its .Net framework, which was developed using other languages like C, C++, and Java as a foundational basis. In 2003, C# became an ISO certified multi-paradigm programming language with powerful features including high functionality, object oriented, imperativeness, declarative attributes and component orientation. Developers use C# a lot to write codes for the XML web services applications as well as Applications connected with Microsoft .Net for the Windows Operating System. The C# language is the go to programming language for Microsoft applications and the language of choice for the Windows Presentation Foundation (WPF). With the introduction of .Net Standard and .Net Core, the .Net ecosystem evolved into cross-platform frameworks and standards, capable of running on Windows, Linux and Mac. The C# language is ideal for beginners and has similar capabilities as Java. It is a high level programming language with high similarity to the English language reading, making it easy to learn and use. It is still not as high level and easy to learn for beginners as Python. Game development is another population application for the C# language, said to be the language of choice to develop and enhance games on the "Unity Game Engine". Developers can write android and iOS applications in C# using Microsoft Xamarin framework.

Java

Java, now owned by Oracle, was introduced in 1991 by Sun Microsystems as a high-level, memory managed language called "Oak" to add capabilities to the C++ language. It is the leading development language and framework with features like general-purpose, object-oriented making it ideal for web based application development. Java runs on the principle of WORA (Write Once Run Anywhere) and has cross-platform capability, making it ideal for developing mobile and gaming applications at the enterprise level.

The Java Server Pages (JSP) is used to develop web based applications. Java allows applications to be accessed through a browser and easily downloadable. The

Java byte code is compiled from the Java language and runs on the Java Virtual Machine (JVM).

These JVMs are available for a majority of operating systems like Windows and Mac. Some programs that are developed using Java are Eclipse, Lotus Notes, Minecraft, Adobe Creative Suite and open office. Google's Android operating system and app development are primarily driven by Java. It is a robust and interpreted language with high application portability, extensive network library and automatic memory management.

JavaScript

Due to a similarity in the name, people often assume that there is an underlying connection to Java, but it's far from the truth. JavaScript was developed in 1995 by the company Netscape and called "LiveScript". JavaScript processes commands on the computer instead of a server and runs inside a client browser. It is primarily used in web development to make webpages more dynamic and manipulate various elements such as: creating a calendar functionality, printing time and date, adding webpage scrolling abilities and other features that cannot be developed using plain HTML.

Web server called NodeJS runs entirely on JavaScript on the server-side. JavaScript is frequently used by front-end web developers and game developers in a variety of domains such as marketing, information technology, engineering, healthcare and finance. A British agency called Cyber-Duck was developed with JavaScript and uses public APIs to access data concerning crime and enable authorities to review and safeguard local areas. Pete Smart and Robert Hawkes created "Tweetmap", that serves as a depiction of the world map in proportion to the number of "tweets" generated by each country. The fundamental features of JavaScript are considered relatively easy to understand and master. A comprehensive JavaScript library called "JQuery" containing multiple frameworks is widely used by the developers as reference.

Python

Python first introduced in 1989 and is touted as extremely user-friendly and easy to learn programming language for amateurs and entry level coders. It is considered perfect for people who have newly taken up interest in programming or coding and need to understand the fundamentals of programming. This emanates from the fact that Python reads almost like English language. Therefore, it requires less time to understand how the language works and focus can be directed in learning the basics of programming.

Here are some of the fundamental elements of computer programming language:

- **Data Type** – This concept is applicable to every programming language ever designed. The data type is simply a representation of the type of data that needs to be processed by the computer. Some of the most common data types are string, numeric, alphanumeric, decimals, among others. Each programming language has its own definition of the data types and keywords used to write the code. For example, the keyword "char" is used to define string data type in C and Java.

- **Variable** – Data values can be stored on a computer by specifying desired label or name to select computer memory locations. These labels are referred to as variables. For instance, you can store values like "Christmas is on" and "12/25" using variables like "A" and "B" and then subsequently execute scientific program to retrieve desired output. Every programming language will have unique keywords and syntax to create and use required variables.

- **Keywords** – Each programming language has a basic syntax with certain words reserved to indicate specific meaning and cannot be used to create variable names. For example, C programming language used words like "int" and "float" to indicate data types; therefore, you will not be able to create variables named "int" or "float".

- **Basic Operators** – Programming language operators refer to symbols that inform the program compiler to perform the indicated mathematical, logical or relational operation and produce desired output. For example, the arithmetic operator "+" in C programming language will execute the addition command on indicated values. Similarly, relational operator ">" will allow you to compare data values and generate true or false result.

• **Decision Making** – This element pertains to selection of one of the provided options on the basis of the provided conditions. For instance, if a remark needs to be printed, the programming code needs to include one or more required conditional statements that will be processed through the workflow of the program. "If" and "If else" conditional statements are some of the decision making statements used in C and Python.

• **Functions** – A set of reusable and organized code that can be utilized to execute a related action is called as function. They offer enhanced modularity for the app and more reusability of the code. For instance, built in functions like "main ()" or "printf ()" can be written and used in C programming language. Different languages refer to functions using different terminologies like subroutine, method, or procedure.

• **File I/O** – Data values can be stored in various formats such as images, plain texts, rich media, and more using computer files. You can organize these files into distinct directories. In short, files hold data and directories hold files. For instance , the extension ".c" will be added to the end of C programming files and extension ".java" to all Java files. The input files can be created in text editing tools like MS Word or Notepad and output files allows reading of the data from the file. The output files are used to show the results on the screen by executing the input to the program from the command prompt.

Importance of Mathematics in Computer Programming

The discipline of mathematics is extremely important to learn and understand the fundamental concepts of computer programming. Various concepts of "Discrete Mathematics", such as probability, algebra, set theory, logic notation, among others, are intricate parts of computer programming. Algebra is frequently used in programming languages. For example, "Boolean Algebra" can be utilized in logical operations and "Relational Algebra" can be utilized in databases. Another example is used of "Number Theory" in the development of cryptocurrency.

Computer science algorithms, including machine learning algorithms, consist of a set of instructions required in the implementation of an application or program. A basic algorithm is as simple as a mathematics statement written using logical operator "+" (5+7 = 12) to code for the addition of data values. The whole concept of data analysis and problem solving is dependent on the mathematical equations that are analyzed to understand the crux of an error. By addressing those issues directly using the mathematics of the program, hard fixes can be easily made to the application.

Statistics is also widely used in data mining and compression, as well as speech recognition and image analysis software. The field of Artificial Intelligence and Machine Learning share a lot of core concepts from the field of statistics. "Statistical learning" is a descriptive statistics-based learning framework that can be categorized as supervised or unsupervised. "Supervised statistical learning" includes constructing a statistical model to predict or estimate output based on single or multiple inputs, on the other hand, "unsupervised statistical learning" involves inputs but no supervisory output, but helps in learning data relationships and structure. One way of understanding statistical learning is to identify the connection between the "predictor" (autonomous variables, attributes) and the "response" (autonomous variable), in order to produce a specific model which is capable of predicting the "response variable (Y)" on the basis of "predictor factors (X)".

"$X = f(X) + \varepsilon$ where $X = (X1, X2, \ldots, Xp)$", where "f" is an *unknown function* & "ε" is *random error (reducible & irreducible)*.

If there are a number of inputs "X" easily accessible, but the output "B" production is unknown, "f" is often treated as a black box, provided that it generates accurate predictions for "Y". This is called "prediction". There are circumstances in which we need to understand how "Y" is influenced as "X" changes. We want to estimate "f" in this scenario, but our objective is not simply to generate predictions for "Y". In this situation, we want to establish and better understand the connection between "Y" and "X". Now "f" is not regarded as a black box since we have to understand the underlying process of the system. This is called "inference". In everyday life, various issues can be categorized into the setting of "predictions", the setting of "inferences", or a "hybrid" of the two.

The "parametric technique" can be defined as an evaluation of "f" by calculating the set parameters (finite summary of the data) while establishing an assumption about the functional form of "f". The mathematical equation of this technique is "$f(X) = \beta 0 + \beta 1 X1 + \beta 2 X2 + \ldots + \beta p X p$". The "parametric models" tend to have a finite number of parameters which is independent of the size of the data set. This is also known as "model-based learning". For example, "k-Gaussian models" are driven by parametric techniques.

On the other hand, the "non-parametric technique" generates an estimation of "f" on the basis of its closeness to the data points, without making any assumptions on the functional form of "f". The "non-parametric models" tend to have a varying number of parameters, which grows proportionally with the size of the data set. This is also known as "memory-based learning". For example, "kernel density models" are driven by a non-parametric technique.

Python Machine Learning: An hands-on introduction to artificial intelligence coding, a project-based guide with practical exercises (Book 2)

This book will discuss the fundamental concepts of machine learning models that can be generated and advanced by utilizing Python based libraries.

The first chapter will introduce you to the core concepts of machine learning as well as various terminologies that are frequently used in this field. It will also provide you a thorough understanding of the significance of machine learning in our daily lives. Some of the most widely used learning models, such as Artificial Neural Networks (ANN) and Genetic Algorithms (GA) are explained in detail in the second chapter.

Chapter 3 will introduce you to the four fundamental machine learning algorithms with explicit details on the supervised machine learning algorithms. The subsequent chapter will include details on various unsupervised machine learning algorithms, such as clustering and dimensionality reduction among others.You will also learn how the raw data can be processed to generate high quality training data set for the production of a successful machine learning model. The sixth chapter of this book will deep dive into the functioning of ML library called Scikit-Learn along with guidance on resolving nonlinear issues with k-nearest neighbor and kernel trick algorithms. The final chapter will explain the nuances of developing a neural network to generate predictions and build the desired machine learning model by utilizing the Tensorflow Python library. We have also provided review exercises to help you test your understanding through this process. Every chapter of this book has real life examples and applications included to solidify your understanding of each concept.

Day 1: Introduction to Machine Learning

The modern concept of Artificial Intelligence technology is derived from the idea that machines are capable of human like intelligence and potentially mimic human thought processing and learning capabilities to adapt to fresh inputs and perform tasks with no human assistance. Machine learning is integral to the concept of artificial intelligence. Machine Learning can be defined as a concept of Artificial Intelligence technology that focuses primarily on the engineered capability of machines to explicitly learn and self-train, by identifying data patterns to improve upon the underlying algorithm and make independent decisions with no human intervention. In 1959, pioneering computer gaming and artificial intelligence expert, Arthur Samuel, coined the term "machine learning" during his tenure at IBM.

Machine learning stems from the hypothesis that modern day computers have an ability to be trained by utilizing targeted training data sets, that can be easily customized to develop desired functionalities. Machine learning is driven by the pattern recognition technique wherein the machine records and revisits past interactions and results that are deemed in alignment with its current situation. Given the fact that machines are required to process endless amounts of data, with new data always pouring in, they must be equipped to adapt to the new data without needing to be programmed by a human, which speaks to the iterative aspect of machine learning.

Now the topic of machine learning is so "hot" that the world of academia, business as well as the scientific community have their own take on its definition. Here are a few of the widely accepted definitions from select highly reputed sources:

- *"Machine learning is the science of getting computers to act without being explicitly programmed".* – Stanford University

- *"The field of Machine Learning seeks to answer the question, "How can we build computer systems that automatically improve with experience, and what are the fundamental laws that govern all learning processes?"* – Carnegie Mellon University

- *"Machine learning algorithms can figure out how to perform important tasks by generalizing from examples".* – University of Washington

- *"Machine Learning, at its most basic, is the practice of using algorithms to parse data, learn from it, and then make a determination or prediction about something in the world".* – Nvidia

- *"Machine learning is based on algorithms that can learn from data without relying on rules-based programming".* – McKinsey & Co.

Core concepts of machine learning

The biggest draw of this technology is its inherent ability of the system to automatically learn programs from the raw data in lieu of manually engineering the program for the machine. Over the last 10 years or so, the application of ML algorithms has expanded from computer science labs to the industrial world. Machine learning algorithms are capable of generalizing tasks so they can be executed iteratively. The process of developing specific programs for specific tasks is extremely taxing in terms of time and money, but occasionally, it is just impossible to achieve. On the other hand, machine learning programming is often feasible and tends to be much more cost effective. The use of machine learning in addressing ambitious issues of widespread importance such as global warming and depleting underground water levels, is promising with massive collection of relevant data.

"A breakthrough in machine learning would be worth ten Microsofts".
– Bill Gates

A number of different types of ML models exist today, but the concept of ML largely boils down to three core components "representation", "evaluation", and "optimization". Here are some of the standard concepts that are applicable to all of them:

Representation

Machine learning models are incapable of directly hearing, seeing, or sensing input examples. Therefore, data representation is required to supply the model with a useful vantage point into the key qualities of the data. To be able to successfully train a machine learning model selection of key features that best represent the data is very important. "Representation" simply refers to the act of representing data points to the computing system in a language that it understands with the use of a set of classifiers. A classifier can be defined as "a system that inputs a vector of discrete and or continuous feature values and outputs a single discrete value called class". For a model to learn from the represented data, the training data set or the "hypothesis space" must contain the desired classifier that you want the models to be trained on. Any classifiers that are external to the hypothesis space cannot be learned by the model. The data features used to represent the input are extremely crucial to the machine learning process. The data features are so critical to the development of the desired machine learning model that it could easily be the key distinction between a successful and failed machine learning project. A training data set consisting of multiple independent feature sets that are well correlated with the class can make the machine learning much smoother. On the other hand, class consisting of complex features may not be easy to learn from for the machine. This usually needs the raw data to be processed to allow the construction of desired features from it, which could then be utilized for the development of the ML model. The process of deriving features from raw data tends to be the most time consuming and laborious part of the ML projects. It is also considered the most creative and exciting part of the project where intuition and trial and error play just as important role as the technical requirements. The process of ML is not a single shot process of developing a training data set and executing it; instead, it's an iterative process that requires analysis of the post run results followed by modification of the training data set and then repeating the whole process all over again. Another contributing factor to the extensive time and effort required in the engineering of the training data set is domain specificity. Training data set for an e-commerce platform to generate predictions based on consumer behavior analysis will be very different from the training data set required to develop a self-driving car. However, the actual machine learning process largely holds true across the industrial spectrum. No wonder, a lot of research is being done to automate the feature engineering process.

Evaluation

Essentially the process of judging multiple hypothesis or models to choose one model over another is referred to as an evaluation. To be able to differentiate between good classifiers from the not so good ones, an "evaluation function" must be used. The evaluation function is also called "objective", "utility", or "scoring" function. The machine learning algorithm has its own internal evaluation function, which tends to be different from the external evaluation function used by the researchers to optimize the classifier. Normally the evaluation function will be defined prior to the selection of the data representation tool and tends to be the first step of the project. For example, the machine learning model for self-driving cars has a feature that allows identification of pedestrians in the car's vicinity at near zero false negatives and a low false positive, which are the evaluation functions and the pre-existing condition that needs to be "represented" using applicable data features.

Optimization

The process of searching the space of presented models to achieve better evaluations or highest scoring classifier is called as "optimization". For algorithms with multiple optimum classifiers, the selection of optimization technique is very important in the determination of the classifier produced as well as to achieve a more efficient learning model. A variety of off-the-shelf optimizers are available in the market that will help you kick start a new machine learning model before eventually replacing them with a custom designed optimizers.

Basic machine learning terminologies

Agent – In context of reinforcement learning, an agent refers to an entity that utilizes a policy to max out the expected return achieved with the transition of different environment states.

Boosting – Boosting can be defined as a ML technique that would sequentially combine set of simple and low accuracy classifiers (known as "weak" classifiers) into a classifier which is highly accurate (known as "strong" classifier) by increasing the weight of the samples that are being classified wrongly by the model.

Candidate generation – The phase of selecting the initial set of suggestions provided by a recommendation system is referred to as candidate generation. For example, a book library can offer 60,000 different books. Through this phase, a subset of few 100 titles meeting the needs of a particular user will be produced and can be refined further to an even smaller set as needed.

Categorical Data – Data features boasting a distinct set of potential values is called as categorical data. For example, a categorical feature named TV model can have a discrete set of multiple possible values, including Smart, Roku, Fire.

Checkpoint – Checkpoint can be defined as a data point that will capture the state of the variables at a specific moment in time of the ML model. With the use of checkpoints, training can be carried out across multiple sessions and model weights or scores can be exported.

Class – Class can be defined as "one of a set of listed target values for a given label". For instance, a model designed to detect junk emails can have 2 different classes, namely, "spam" and "not spam".

Classification model – The type of machine learning model used to differentiate between multiple distinct classes of the data is referred to as a classification model. For example, a classification model for identification of dog breeds could assess whether the dog picture used as input is Labrador, Schnauzer, German Shepherd, Beagle and so on.

Collaborative filtering – The process of generating predictions for a particular user based on the shared interests of a group of similar users is called collaborative filtering.

Continuous feature – It is defined as a "floating point feature with an infinite range of possible values".

Discrete feature – It is defined as a feature that can be given only a finite set of potential values and has no flexibility.

Discriminator – A system used to determine whether the input samples are realistic or not is called as discriminator.

Down-sampling – The process of Down-sampling refers to the process used to reduce the amount of info comprised in a feature or use of an extremely low percentage of classes that are abundantly represented in order to train the ML model with higher efficiency.

Dynamic model – A learning model that is continuously receiving input data to be trained in a continuous manner is called a dynamic model.

Ensemble – A set of predictions created by combining predictions of more than one model is called an ensemble.

Environment – The term environment used in the context of reinforcement machine learning constitutes "the world that contains the agent and allows the agent to observe that world's state".

Episode – The term episode used in the context of reinforcement machine learning constitutes every sequential trial taken by the model to learn from its environment.

Feature – Any of the data variables that can be used as an input to generate predictions is called a feature.

Feature engineering – Feature engineering can be defined as "the process of determining which features might be useful in training a model, and then converting raw data from log files and other sources into said features".

Feature extraction – Feature extraction can be defined as "the process of retrieving intermediate feature representations calculated by an unsupervised or pre-trained model for use in another model as input".

Few-shot learning - Few-shot learning can be defined as "a machine learning approach, often used for object classification, designed to learn effective classifiers from only a small number of training examples".

Fine tuning – The process of "performing a secondary optimization to adjust the parameters of an already trained model to fit a new problem" is called as fine tuning. It is widely used to refit the weight(s) of a "trained unsupervised model" to a "supervised model".

Generalization – A machine learning model's capability to produce accurate predictions from fresh and unknown input data instead of the data set utilized during the training phase of the model is called generalization.

Inference – In context of ML, inference pertains to the process of generating predictions and insight with the application of an already trained model to unorganized data sample.

Label – In context of machine learning (supervised), the "answer" or "result" part of an example is called a label. Each title in a labeled dataset will consist of single or multiple features along with a label. For example, in a house data set, the features could contain the year built, number of rooms and bathrooms, while the label can be the "house's price".

Linear model – Linear model is defined as a model that can assign singular weight to each feature for generating predictions.

Loss – In context of ML, loss pertains to the measure of the extent by which the predictions produced by the model are not in line with its training labels.

Matplotlib – It is an "open source Python 2-D plotting library" that can be utilized to visualize various elements of ML.

Model – In context of ML, a model refers to a representation of the learning and training that has been acquired by the system from the training dataset.

NumPy – It is an open sourced data library that can provide effective operations to be used on Python arrays.

One-shot learning – In context of machine learning, one-shot learning can be defined as the machine learning approach that allows learning of effective classifiers from unique training sample and is frequently utilized classification of objects.

Overfitting - In context of machine learning, overfitting is referred to as production of a model that can match the training dataset extremely closely and renders the model inefficient in making accurate predictions on fresh input.

Parameter – Any variable of the ML model, which would allow the machine learning system to self-learn independently is called parameter.

Pipeline – In context of ML, pipeline pertains to the infrastructure that surrounds a learning algorithm and comprises of a collection of data, any data additions made to the training data files, training of single or multiple models, and releasing the models into live environment.

Random forest – In context of machine learning, the concept of random forest pertains to an ensemble technique to find a decision tree that would most accurately fit the training dataset by creating two or more decision trees with a random selection of features.

Scaling - In context of machine learning, scaling refers to "a common feature engineering practice to tame a feature's range of values to match the range of other features in the dataset".

Sequence model - A sequence model simply refers to a model with sequential dependency on data inputs to generate a future prediction.

If you enjoyed this preview be sure to check out the full books on Amazon.com. Complete the journey and become a Python master!

Conclusion

Thank you for making it through to the end of *Python Data Science: An hands-on introduction to big data analysis and data mining, a project-based guide with practical exercises (Book 3)*, let's hope it was informative and able to provide you with all of the tools you need to achieve your goals whatever they may be.

The next step is to make the best use of your new-found wisdom on the cutting-edge data science technologies like "Big Data Analytics" and Data mining across the industrial spectrum. The smart and savvy customers today can be easily swayed by modern companies with a whimsical edge offering consumers a unique, rich, and engaging experience. It is getting increasingly challenging for traditional businesses to retain their customers without adopting the big data analytics technology explained in this book. You are now ready to make your own predictive analysis model by leveraging all the free and open-source data libraries described in this book. You now have an overview of the application of AI technology in the marketing space with AI based tools like "GetResponse Autofunnel" that have automated the traditional process of creating industry and business-specific marketing funnels to attract new customers or prospective leads and convert them into paying customers. As a business leader, you must keep current on tools and technologies that can help you grow and expand your businesses and as you will learn with the help of this book the future lies within the girth of cutting-edge technologies like AI, Machine learning and big data analytics. So we have provided an in-depth explanation of what is big data and how modern day analytical tools and technologies can be applied on this treasure of data to gain invaluable insights and take your business to the next level. By the time you're finished reading this book, you would be familiar with some of the most popular computer programming languages and machine learning libraries that you can selectively incorporate within your company's software platforms, to improve your sales and gain more profit. To make the best use of this book, I recommend that you download these free resources and perform hands-on exercises to solidify your understanding of the concepts explained. The skillset of data analysis is always in demand, with a lot of high pay job opportunities. Here's hoping this book has taken you a step closer to your dream job!